Contents

1. Forward — 1
2. Why This Book — 7
   Take What Resonates and Leave the Rest
   What Is This "Source" You Keep Talking About?
3. Step 1 - Awaken — 19
   Changes I've Experienced Since Awakening
   A Neurobiological Shift Takes Place When You Awaken
   Your Kundalini Goes Into Orbit
   In Awakening's Early Phases, Your Mind will Likely Work Against You
   Japa – A Fun Exercise to Help Embody Your True Nature
   Thoughts are an Environment Unto Themselves
   Receive Awakening
   Fully Awakening May Take Some Time

4. Step 2 - Clear Emotional Blockages — 74
   Why Fully Experiencing Emotions Is Important
   Getting to the Root Cause of a Trapped Emotion
   How to Clear Emotional Charges
   Stories of Transformation
   Resources to Help

5. Step 3 - Invite Your Sacred Higher Self Into Your Life — 138
   Make Your Divine Your Best Friend
   The Parable of Your New Neighbor
   What It Looks Like When Your Higher Self Is Your Best Friend
   The Game Plan
   Are You Ready to Channel?
   Setting Your Boundaries

6. Living An Ascended Life — 168
   Laugh
   Work Less, Allow More
   Let Go of Attending to Problems in the World
   Find Your Tribe

7. Peter's Bio — 190

Forward

There're a lot of channeled books written, offering great teachings and hope. This book is unique in that it does more than carry a message of upliftment. This book is written to offer you a helping hand as you step across the gap between the third and fifth densities. My intent is to offer simple steps you can take to aid your Ascension.

Earth's Ascension will see the planet and its inhabitants move from 3D to 5D. Essentially this means your vibration will become less dense. We're not talking about dimensions. We're talking about energetic densities that consciousness inhabits. You see, consciousness is the whole game. In 3D, the energetic field is more compressed. In 5D we vibrate at "higher" frequencies. And with this new vibrational resonance underpinning "reality," everything as we know it will change.

The practices outlined here are ones I have personally used to great result in the spiritual growth that embodies my Ascension. I've also seen many others use these steps to effectively transition into greater awareness and more expanded consciousness. These steps are replicable. I've done it. I've seen others do it. And now guidance from my Sacred Higher Self is asking me to share these steps with you.

Everything written here is colored by the flavor of my Sacred Higher Self. Because I've been in 24-7 contact with my Spirit for a while now, it's hard to distinguish when it's the me I know as my 3D self talking, when it's my Higher Self, and when it's the merging of the two, which has my 5D self/Sacred Higher Self driving the bus. This kind of constant contact with the Divine is where we're all headed. I'm proud I get to be part of the movement to demonstrate and provide steps to help guide you toward the awesome state of being you'll enjoy when you meld with your Sacred Higher Self.

This book has three main parts:

- Step 1: Awaken
- Step 2: Clear Emotional Blockages
- Step 3: Invite Your Sacred Higher Self Into Your Life

Though they are presented in a numbered order, the steps will work best when you work them all at the same time. Once you understand a step and begin to practice it, try to make time in your life to begin practicing another step. Don't wait until you feel you've "mastered" a step before you begin another.

Each of these steps will begin with a description that introduces the concept so you can create a mental space for your awareness to become familiar with and eventually embrace that teaching. The descriptions will be followed by how-to steps that will allow you to embody it.

If you're interested in my bona fides, you can read my bio in the back of this book. Or you can visit becomingawesome.one to learn more. But the story of how I started my Ascension and the skills I've been blessed with along the way are not what's important here. What's important is whether or not you resonate with the energy of these words. Above all else, claim your sovereignty by making choices based on your own inner knowing. If you felt drawn to this book, you're definitely in the right place. If not, please check in with yourself to be clear before investing your time and effort practicing the steps presented.

And in case you're wondering, I'm able to channel. I can communicate with any entity I can identify. Everything I present in this book has been run past my Sacred Higher Self to make sure it's properly aligned. And when I write about Source itself, I ask God to provide the words. As you develop your own abilities to communicate with Spirit, please be sure to check in with Source and verify these teachings for yourself. Think of your receiving internal confirmation your graduation ceremony.

My path has been an amalgamation of schools like Oneness University and the Ramtha School of Enlightenment. Teachers like Kryon, channeled by Lee Carroll, and Abraham, channeled by Esther Hicks. I've also taken classes and done intensive self-study of works by GW Hardin, Joe Dispenza, Inelia Benz and books like *Right Use of Will*. Everything presented here is a synthesis of all these and information I've gleaned from many other esteemed teachers. The processes presented are either self-discovered or tweaked versions of those taught by the giants I'm standing on the shoulders of. What's important for you to understand is that there's no one right way to do Ascension. My goal in writing this book is to distill the most practical parts of my life experience and present them in an easy way so that you can learn the basics and move quickly into your own Ascension. Here's a big THANK YOU to every teacher I've had the pleasure of sitting at the feet of.

I am also eternally grateful to the mentors who have been in my life. Robert O. Weiss, Tom Benson and, especially, GW Hardin. My wife, Tracy Juechter, has been my greatest love and one of my wisest teachers, and contributed substantially to the content of this book. I'm in awe with gratitude that I get to live with her and enjoy her support as my journey called me to commit to full-time service.

And I have to thank Elan, which is a group consciousness I'm a member of. Much love and guidance has come to me from Elan and from all the members of my weekly Elan meditation circle. Elan was created by my meditation circle, which evolved over years of being in Oneness together. We asked our higher selves and divine teams to merge with each other, thereby giving the whole circle access to the entire team. The entity that got created from that request let us know it could be called Elan.

I'll be detailing the steps for creating and participating in your own group consciousness in the third book of this three-part series. For now, focus on mastering the skills presented here. It will make creating a group consciousness and the other skills presented in *My Ascension Handbooks Level II* and *Level III* easier for you to receive.

I'd also like to give credit and appreciation to the readers who helped refine and improve on the material presented here: Tracy Juechter and JoAnna Stansby. On the nonphysical side, I'm smitten with love and gratitude for my soul, which I call my Sacred Higher Self. I've also been friends with and have received important teachings and guidance from Sekhmet and her Siriuan kin Cheops and Knute, Mira and Selana from the Pleiades, Celestus from Oneness, the 9D Arcturian Council, and Archangel Michael, among others.

And while on the topic of where this information comes from, it's important to say a big THANK YOU to everyone who came before me to open these pathways of knowledge. Some of it is ancient wisdom. Some comes from the monks and teachers listed above. Some from many other people who showed up in my life to speak the words of God in the right way, at the right time, so I could receive it. And some comes directly from Source, through my Sacred Higher Self, who is helping me to write this book. My gratitude runs deep! Only once before in my life have words flowed onto the page with such ease and grace as they do now as I write.

Thank you, more please!

One final note before we begin. Be sure to check out my website becomingawesome.one for more tools and resources. There's a wealth of free processes available, and a link where you can sign up for personal coaching or clearing sessions on a donation basis. We'll also be offering free online Q&As and energetic transmissions for Awakening from time to time. And there are full weekend online classes covering all the teachings and group process versions of the steps in this book. These classes offer the opportunity for you to immerse yourself in the steps covered in this book, and to do so in a group energy field of consciousness that will make your ability to transform even stronger. Please visit becomingawesome.one/events for more details.

Many blessings to you – Peter D.

Why This Book

You're aware the Golden Age has dawned. You've probably begun to notice subtle changes in your interests and demeanor. You may have heard that Earth is Ascending, but you're not really sure what that means. You're part of the next wave of people who are beginning their Ascension journey.

Ascension is a catch-all word that many people are talking about and few can give a specific definition to. It's basically a combination of what happens when you become Awakened, enlightened and God-realized. Yes, it's all of that — having the wisdom, presence and abilities of saints, sages and ascended masters. And you're in line to become this.

One of the characteristics of the 3D world we grew up in is separation. The density of the energy in 3D makes it difficult for our perception fields to extend much beyond our bodies and its physical senses. So even though we are self-aware beings, nearly all of us see ourselves as separate in that awareness.

Some of us take this separation to the extreme of thinking our consciousness is only a one-time deal, believing that we're born, we die, and that's it. Game over. Consciousness extinguished.

Nearly 90 percent of people on the planet see more to their lives. They believe in souls, an afterlife, or reincarnation. But even many of the people who believe they have an eternal soul, separate themselves by believing that Heaven is a place you go to that's somewhere else. Or that your soul may have experienced other "lives," but such knowledge is something that only a very few "special" people can access.

As you move into 5D your beliefs about reality and who and what you are will expand. They have to. Because moving into 5D means you fully embrace that you are a consciousness. This awareness becomes rooted in your thoughts. It changes the unconscious programming governing your perceptions and reactions. You'll find yourself drawn to take different actions. And you'll be happier when you do.

Most of us were born in 3D. And whether you realize it or not, Earth's transformation into 5D is a big, big deal. It's the first time the population of a planet has ascended all at once (really within a few generations) in our galaxy. Historically, we have reports of a small handful of people ascending in their lifetime. The Western Bible speaks of Elijah and Ezekiel doing so. Eastern scriptures speak of ascended masters. But people of this caliber being present on the planet at the same time have been few and far between.

Things are changing now. We're all now able to ascend and stay physically on the planet in our bodies. And the fact that you're here for this experience of Ascension is huge. Your soul did not just willy-nilly show up for this momentous shift because it was bored and wanted some entertainment. You're here because it's time for you to embrace the magnificence of who you are and begin to embody it, moving 5D energies into your physical body—literally bringing Heaven to Earth. And especially for those of us who will be among the first to enjoy mass Ascension, it is likely you will feel called to help Earth and other people as they uplift. Everything is changing and those of us with awareness of the nature of this change are ready to become the first wave of current-day embodied masters, allowing us to help many others ascend.

This profound transformation is not just taking place in the spiritual realm. It's physically observable for those with eyes to see. Check how the Schumann resonances, which measure the Earth's resonant fields, are orders of magnitude above what science declared was normal just a few decades ago. Or look at the activity of solar flares and storms. They're off the charts as well. Global warming isn't just happening on Earth. NASA data shows every planet in our solar system is warming up.

And did you know the galaxy not only spins, it wobbles? For the past few decades our arm of the galaxy has been passing through the center line of the galactic plane. And it's doing so while our arm of the galaxy (and the whole galaxy itself) is moving through more energetically active regions of space.

These scientifically observable phenomena coincide with indigenous prophecies all across the globe. You may have heard about the Mayan calendar, which predicts the end of time as we know it. But dozens of other traditions speak of the Golden Age coming to Earth at this time. Some of the Hindu Vedas lay out twenty-six-thousand-year cycles (which just happen to be the same time span as our galactic wobble). Their teachings say we are leaving the twenty-six-thousand-year Kali Yuga—the Iron Age—where humans are separated and destructive. We are now moving into the Satya Yuga—the Golden Age. It is a time where we'll understand we are made with and of the essence of God. Our connections to the Divine will be so palpable, we'll know ourselves to be God-realized.

My Ascension Handbook – Level I is the first of a three-part series, written to give you simple, practical steps can take to make your Ascension as smooth and quick as possible. This book focuses on how to have a clear, continuous connection with your soul—or your Sacred Higher Self as I call it. And I'm not just talking about awareness that you are a soul, or book learning about souls, or even knowledge of saints and sages who've performed miracles because they were able to connect to their Spirit. I'm talking about you, in a very real sense, being able to speak with your Sacred Higher Self and hear responses clear as day in return. And with this type of connection, you'll be able to speak with and channel any other conscious entity, from the great masters to ETs to deceased loved ones and more. This book is about the first steps on your path to reaching a clear continuous connection with your Higher Self.

Book II will carry your skills further by providing tools you can use to achieve God-realization. Yes, full knowledge and embodiment of you as a Source Energy Being, including the ability to see, or know, any event or information in the universe because you'll have access to it through your expansive connection to All That Is.

Book III will show you the steps for creating group consciousness and focus on ways you can be in service by helping others receive the Ascension abilities you've learned in the first two books. You see, as your consciousness expands to understand that you are a Source Energy Being, you'll find that service is one of the greatest pleasures and sources of fulfillment. It's why I'm writing these books. Helping others advance in their Ascension is literally one of the few things that excites me these days. And of course, I'm selfish. I've learned that the quickest way to receive miracles in my life is to help others have miracles in theirs.

If you have not already received it. Let me be the first to formally welcome you to the Golden Age. Welcome to the awesome journey of consciously embracing your Ascension!

Take What Resonates and Leave the Rest

This book is written from my personal experience and is guided by the direction of my Sacred Higher Self. I was a seeker for many years, and until I received Awakening, I never found anything that filled the uncomfortable void I had within myself. Now Spirit is asking me to share what I've learned, especially the how-to steps for getting here. The techniques I'm offering are what has worked for me, and what my Sacred Higher Self envisions will work for those of you reading this. (And yes, my Source is in the Oneness field with your Source and knows who you are. And that connection with you is directing the guidance given to me about what to write. Crazy, huh?)

The most important advice I can give you as you proceed with learning and using the tools in this book is to trust yourself. If something feels right for you, it is. If it doesn't feel right, see if it's triggering an emotional blockage in you that needs to be cleared (more on this later in Step 2 – Clearing Emotional Blockages). And if it still doesn't feel right, then let it go. It's not for you. Finding your energetic match is critical to your Ascension. There are many roads that will lead you to yours. This is not the only way. Trust yourself!

Please don't compare teachers, schools, traditions, lineages or religions. They all individually work for those in alignment with their chosen path. Here's how you can take another step toward your Ascension and sovereignty right now: Keep an open mind as you read this book. Don't think of this as a scholarly or scientific work that is supposed to be documented, proven in controlled experiments, or accepted by religious leaders. Your intuition led you to this book. Trust it. Give what you read a try and see what you experience. Then you'll have certain knowledge if this is working for you. If what you read resonates on some level, you're in the right place. If not, then not. As one teacher of mine used to say, "You make your choices and you live with them." Own that you're in charge of your choices. Take responsibility for what you are choosing, for how you're relating to the material in this book. Claiming your power is foundational for stepping into your Ascension.

Ascension is largely uncharted territory. If there was a simple way to get there already available, we'd all already be ascended and going on our merry way. Nearly everything we've been taught so far in our lives no longer applies. Even basic things like right and wrong. The oil no longer floats on the water. In 5D it's mixed among it. The oil is a part of the water. Expanding your consciousness means expanding your viewpoints and beliefs. You can't have one without the other.

The only thing I can say for certain is that my life has changed radically as I've been living more and more in 5D. I'm happier, healthier, more motivated and excited to be alive. And I am continually taking great pleasure in almost every little thing I experience. I can channel. I am being guided toward better and better situations and outcomes. I am starting to dance through timelines. And I have pretty much mastered the ability to know what I need to know when I need to know it. Abundance is flowing to me at all times—talk about reasons for being grateful, eh? Thank you, sweet Divine!

And as my joy and fulfillment levels increase, I'm called more and more to share this with everyone ready to embrace their Ascension. I can't promise you that what's written here will get you where I'm at, but I can tell you with certainty that it's worked for me. And my Sacred Higher Self is telling me through a loudspeaker to share this with the world. Here's one simple set of steps that worked for me, my wife, those I regularly meditate with and many people I've given clearing and coaching sessions to. If the energy feels right to you, then it is. Trust this will work for you.

What Is This "Source" You Keep Talking About?

"God," "Source," "Divine" and other terms referring to "Universal Intelligence" are used interchangeably in this book. You see, this book is not about religion. Ascension is for everyone, regardless of their religion. And no matter their spiritual belief system. We're all on this ride together, even though every single person on the planet approaches it differently.

The bottom line is we're all going to experience some degree of unity consciousness when we're in 5D. We're going to feel connected in deeply fulfilling ways that words cannot describe. The field of connection we'll be in will have every type of entity and consciousness you can imagine, and many more yet to be revealed. What is this field? And what are these wonderfully unique bits of consciousness in them that I call entities? Some people describe it as the "All That Is," which is another great name for Source.

You see, if God is truly the Alpha and the Omega, as the Western Bible describes it, then everything in between is also God. If God made the heavens and the earth, then what did he make them out of? Was there creation before God? If not, then the heavens and the Earth must be made out of God stuff. This means you and I are made out of the very essence of God itself. We're God Source Beings.

Many people drawn to Ascension are finding the spiritual teachings they've been raised with are no longer cutting it. They're looking for something more as their practices have only taken them so far. This book is not trying to offer a new religion. Rather, my intention is to celebrate all religious practices. Use and practice religion if it helps you feel closer to your Source. If not, let go of those teachings/beliefs that keep you from allowing a direct connection to your sacred essence. God doesn't care what you call it. God cares that your call it.

The bottom line is that God indwells you. "Made in God's image" is just another way of saying "made with, by and of God."

One way to understand this conundrum is to look at fractals.

Even though each leaf of this fern is different, it has the same pattern as every other leaf and the entire plant. A fractal contains all the information of that which it is a part of. A tiny seed contains the pattern of the mighty tree it will grow into. We are fractals of God. As such, we have the innate ability to connect with Source in profound ways. The blueprint for doing so is built in. But like a seed, it needs the right environment to grow—fertile soil, mild weather, water and nutrients. In entering the Satya Yuga, our planet is completing a twenty-six-thousand-year cycle. The spiral that is the Milky Way galaxy both rotates and wobbles. We're entering an area of space with a less dense vibrational energy, which gives us more fertile soil to grow into.

Another way of putting it is the veils are lifting. We're starting to become aware that our very reality is a field of consciousness—and it's all connected. Though we are but one leaf, we are also the tree and also the environment in which the tree grows. We are literally a piece of God, blessed with the unique consciousness that you call you. We're fractals of All That Is.

Imagine religion for a moment to be like food. Some people prefer steak. Some prefer vegan. Source is benevolent. It wants to be in connection with you and for you to be in connection with It. When Source invites you over to dinner, it's going to serve your favorite food, so it can better relate to you and make you happy. For some people it serves up Christianity. Some people are served Hinduism. Others receive Islam. You get the idea. All these traditions lead back to Source, because at their heart they're just culturally acceptable ways of describing the relationship of each leaf to the tree.

What this book does is take the next step. Many religions hint at Ascension, but few speak directly about it—let alone give practical steps for achieving it. The bottom line is that you have a personal relationship with your Divine. And it's unique to you. Dive in whatever way is right for you. Ascension is an inner journey. You're on your way to better knowing the

God that dwells within. Call it whatever makes you happy. Build on the foundation your religion has laid for you to stand on. Just be open to allowing new teachings to grow from the fields you've cultivated. If you really wanted the same old, same old, you wouldn't be reading this book. So relax. This book is about you deepening the relationship you have with your personal Divine. To come into clear, continuous contact with your Sacred Higher Self necessarily means deepening your relationship with God. You are a fractal of your Sacred Higher Self, which is a fractal of God.

Enjoy the expansiveness of your true nature as you embrace your Ascension!

Step 1 – Awaken

Awakening is a profound shift in being that takes place as part of Ascension. It happens on a biochemical level in your body and a perceptual level in your consciousness. An Awakened person is authentic. You'll notice it when they speak, because you feel a palpable sense of emotional honesty about them. Awakened people don't pay much attention to social norms. They'll be marching to the beat of their own Divine no matter how odd that seems to those around them.

Becoming Awakened is a beautifully liberating experience and it's yours to receive.

In popular culture, awakening has come to mean becoming savvy as to how the media, financial, political, health and educational systems have been co-opted by a cabal bent on control through fear and misery. This is one truthful analysis of the old energy systems that are dissolving as higher frequency energies of the Golden Age take hold. But other than knowing what's shifting externally, the popular understanding of being awakened has little bearing on your Ascension. And in fact, letting go of focusing on the external changes is key to allowing your Awakening to blossom.

It's easy to be emotionally attached to and focused on the many problems around us. But that attachment actually works against you releasing your own density in order to receive Awakening and to ascend. As we will discuss in Step 2 – Clearing Emotional Blockages, societal problems can act as cues to trigger the release of your trapped emotions around fear, the lack of money or survival. But if you continually focus on that realm, your mind will simply reprogram you to stay in that lower vibration and you'll continue to experience the burden of those problems.

It's kind of like what the law of attraction teaches. What you focus on, expands. Another way to put it is to understand this mantra:

I AM THAT

Since Ascension moves us into more Oneness, the uplifting energies make this even more true. In plain English, I Am That means we become what we love. We become what we hate. We become that which we give our attention to.

Rather than fret and worry about all the evils in the world now being exposed, an Awakened person will instead release their trapped emotions and the unconscious programming that is triggered by them. Once you do, you'll be vibrationally lighter and happier. You'll start to envision and therefore attract a better world—the Golden Age will come to you instead of you having to fight to create it.

The more you ascend, the more you create a bubble of Heaven around you. The energy field you generate starts to transform the world around you and everyone you interact with. Your upliftment uplifts others. That's how the world changes. It's OK to recognize how corrupt things have become in the Kali Yuga, but the battle to change them is an inside job. An Awakened person has healed the traumas within themselves that are reflected to them in the external world.

Here's an example of how your Awakening transforms others. I had never met Kristen before she called me. She did not show up for one of the online clearing sessions that I offer on a donation basis on becomingawesome.one. I had emailed her letting her know she missed it and could reschedule. She called me to apologize. Later that evening I received this email:

> *I have to tell you that I had this amazing thing happen while and just after I talked with you today. I had this very strong sense of well-being and happiness that lasted quite some time after the call. Even as I write this, I am feeling more balanced than I have in over a decade. I have no idea if it was just coincidental, if hearing your voice just gave me some hope and positive anticipation of our upcoming session to clear trapped emotions, or if it was something coming from you. All I can say is THANK YOU!! I have felt a lightness of being all day*

since your call and it has given me hope ... Thank you for your patience and understanding about today. It is much appreciated. I very much look forward to meeting you online next Thursday and again, thank you for that wonderful dose of positivity this morning!!
Kirsten Donald • Ladera Ranch, California

My friends and I who have meditated regularly since 2010 keep track of the Awakening changes we notice in ourselves and each other. We have all had people say things like, "I feel so much calmer around you." Most of us have had coworkers pop into our offices or classrooms just to hang around. When asked about why they're there, most say, "No reason, it just feels good in here."

This is the power the internal shift toward Awakening has on the external world. Most of us want to save the world. We haven't realized until now that it means saving ourselves and then watching the world naturally align with its own salvation. You're a powerful Source Energy Being. Embrace it.

The bottom line is that we are all one. Ascension into 5D means experiencing Oneness. You're connected to God just as you are connected to all those you label as evil-doers. Heal the pain of that evil within yourself and it automatically permeates the field and heals them. This kind of awareness is a major step up in consciousness. So don't get down on yourself for wanting to smack the person you've demonized as the biggest bane to humanity. Given your state of consciousness, there's really no other reaction you can have. There's no blame to be had. I'm presenting this concept here so you can begin to unravel the mystery of Ascension. The material in this chapter will better explain what Awakening is. It will give your mind a place of possibility that will allow Awakening to come to you. After the description of Awakening, we'll outline practical steps you can take to receive Awakening for yourself.

Changes I've Experienced Since Awakening

Awakening was given to me by Sri Bhagavan, the great being who founded Oneness University in Southeastern India. He taught and initiated the monks teaching there, who in turn have passed the blessing of Awakening to many people like me who have been initiated as Oneness Blessing Givers.

My life changed radically the evening I received it. When I woke up the next morning, I was stunned by how much sharper everything looked. All the colors were brighter around me. My wife, who had also received it, kept telling me all the scents of the flowers and trees were so much more fragrant. And we both experienced a deeper connection with nature. Just being on the lawn walking between buildings on campus felt like being in a cathedral with a palpable sense of wonder and awe all around us.

When I returned home, I found that my work efficiency had improved. I was completing work tasks that used to take an hour in twenty minutes or a half hour. Much of this was because my mind was so much quieter. I wasn't nearly as distracted by my mind as I worked. Sure, thoughts would come up about things I was working on. But I was simply aware of those thoughts, not taken in by them. I'd see them arise, but before they could gain any traction or spill into a plethora of other "related" thoughts, they would dissipate. Kind of like noticing the buzzing of a fly in the room for a moment, but not paying attention to it. My focus remained on my work task. Consequently, I completed brain work projects in about a third of the time they used to take.

Another amazing benefit was how connected I became to everyone around me. It first hit me at a grocery store shortly after returning home. I would look at the other shoppers and both see and feel what was going on for them. I could read the emotions they were holding in the moment, and have an inkling of why. My first reaction was to be frightened. I had enough of my own problems I had been avoiding in life. Why in the world would I want to be aware of other people's problems? But I've since realized what an incredible gift this aspect of Oneness is. As long as I don't get stuck in the mental constructs of my own making, I can accurately discern what's going on with others around me. I know when someone is lying. I know when someone believes they are doing a good thing, but there's really an underlying emotional blockage driving their behavior, so that regardless of their intent, the actions they're taking bear bitter fruit.

Most importantly I have compassion like I've never had before. I can literally feel their pain if I choose. It allows me to be empathic and offer guided coaching and healing as I do on my website. And it has tempered my compassion with wisdom. Knowing when a person is coming from an authentic expression of their passion, as opposed to a need to compensate for an unconscious blocked emotion, allows me to know when to steer clear of a person and when to invite them to come closer.

And how's this for a wild result of my Awakening into Oneness? I now know things about my food. When I'm shopping for it, or sitting down to eat, I can "pray" over my meal. I then know how it was grown or raised. I can sense any strong emotions from the people who prepared, packaged or transported it. If I choose, I can feel how the plant or animal was treated when it was killed or harvested. Praying over my food is blessing it by experiencing all the pains carried by that food and then completing the stuck emotional energies attached to it. Things like the pain of when the animal was killed or the plant was cut down. Or how the truck driver transporting it got into a fight that day and unconsciously dosed the food with suppressed rage. Or how the cook felt while stirring the soup. Blessing my food becomes the act of briefly acknowledging all of this, and then using compassion to complete the painful experiences of the heavier energies so they can detach and return to Source. All that's left on my plate after doing this is the blissful Oneness I share with my food and my body as it ingests it.

An even crazier result of my Awakening has been having to let go of all my previous notions of right and wrong. All the old 3D energies of teaching ethics, having moral codes and even the newfangled concepts of being woke simply don't apply anymore. Later in this chapter I will describe how your mind can quiet and you'll be able to become friends with your mind, instead of letting it run the show of your life like you're a puppet. Once you achieve this aspect of Awakening, you'll start to notice how much of the moral and social codes you were raised with simply don't apply. You'll be open to guidance directly from Source instead of relying on the ethical teachings you've memorized.

Take the story a monk shared about a small, elderly woman at a bus stop in India. At the time, the sight of a man beating his wife in public was common there. On her way to work, a man who was much younger, bigger and stronger than her was hitting his wife. Without thinking, she walked over to the man and slapped him. The man instantly fell to his knees, began crying and begging for forgiveness.

There was no worry or fear about the consequences of her action. There was no moral judgment about the right or wrong of what he was doing, or thinking about the ethics of meeting violence with violence. She just did it because she was Awakened and allowed Source to move through her body.

And because she was connected to Source in this way, what she did was appropriate for that man. It changed him and his relationship with his wife.

As you Awaken, all of your relationships will change. I don't have many friends, though the friendships I do have are much deeper. My wife and I still fight from time to time. But half the time the fights are over in a couple of minutes. One of us blurts out why we're angry, and the other one is able to really hear it. We quickly end up seeing in ourselves the blocked emotions we have triggering the event and then know we can process them (as explained in step 2) and then move back into the connected Oneness field of bliss in which we normally interact.

And as described earlier, you becoming Awakened affects those around you. It allows you to generate a field that helps to Awaken anyone you come in contact with. Let's dive a little deeper into understandings that will help you receive Awakening.

A Neurobiological Shift Takes Place When You Awaken

Think about what happens when you have an experience. Once the experience starts, where does your mind go? Many people automatically remember a similar experience, like that thing that happened when you were twelve. Or that really great movie that had a great scene like it. Or a lyric from a song. Or an important book you read where the author said ...

You get the picture. Few unawakened people stay with the experience they are having. Their mind intervenes and they experience a thought or a memory instead of what is taking place in the moment. Like when you're in a conversation and you're thinking about what you're going to say next instead of listening to what the other person is saying and perhaps even feeling the emotions that their words are stirring in you.

This way of being is what most people on the planet have lived with for thousands of years. Our localized minds have become so prominent in our existence that many people unconsciously play old tapes of memories and past thoughts rather than staying present with the experiences they are having. What happens when a person Awakens is that a gap forms between the time they perceive an experience and when their mind kicks in to tell them what to make of it.

This gap is only about four-tenths of a second long. But that's enough. As you move into deeper and deeper levels of Awakening, your mind will become quieter. You'll be having an experience and begin to respond to it, to feel the emotion stirred by it. Then when your mind kicks in—which it usually does—you'll notice it as something outside the experience. You'll be able to unconsciously say to your mind, "Thank you for interrupting but I'm going to stay with this experience for now." And you'll be able to complete the experience by fully feeling what's being triggered. You'll be responding rather than reacting to events in your life.

Your Kundalini Goes Into Orbit

You're probably familiar with your chakras. They're energy centers in your body. Nadis are the channels connecting them. Many New Age practices address clearing and balancing your chakras. Kundalini is life force energy, or as I prefer to call it, Source force energy. Some breath work techniques focus on how your Kundalini moves through your chakras. These often seek to raise your Kundalini through your chakras into your third eye or crown chakra.

When your Kundalini is elevated you can't help but feel great! You'll feel vibrant, more "alive." Things around you will seem to glow. You'll sense being more connected. And your mental acuity will go up a notch. This is what is called being in an Awakened state. You've experienced at least once in your life.

Awakened states, however, are not permanent. They come and they go. Some can last weeks or months, but then fade. Have you ever taken a workshop that left you feeling totally energized? One where you felt ready to take on the world and all its problems? One where you'd swear (at the time) that the people you were with were your soul brothers and sisters? That workshop was able to create energies, connections and teachings that raised your Kundalini. It put you in an

Awakened state. But when you got back to your "normal" life, how long did it last?

For unawakened people, Kundalini can be like a yo-yo. It will rise and fall. You may be seeking out experiences that help raise your Kundalini so you can once again experience those moments of enlightenment (where you are literally lighter) because your Kundalini is so high. When you Awaken, you're permanently in this state. Living with raised Kundalini becomes your new baseline. It's why so many people stop "seeking" and taking workshops once they Awaken. Their lives are constantly flowing with as much energy, connection and mental acuity as they choose to allow.

In addition to the neurobiological shift that causes the gap between experience and your mind's interruption, Awakening involves a person's Kundalini going into orbit. Instead of rising, staying there for a while and then falling, once you're Awakened your Kundalini will rise up to your crown chakra and then cycle around you in a torus back to your root chakra to begin again its climb back up your core to your crown.

Your Kundalini is already doing this to some degree. If it didn't you wouldn't be alive. But when you are fully Awakened, you'll be aware of the flow of your Source force energy. And if you care to, you'll feel it circulate through the orbit of the energetic torus that is your energy body. Know that as you do this, you will be receiving physical evidence of your Awakening. The stronger it becomes, the more Awakened you'll be.

In Awakening's Early Phases, Your Mind will Likely Work Against You

Before learning how you can receive Awakening, let's take a moment to explore some of the pitfalls our minds can create that undermine being in an Awakened state. Let's begin by understanding the difference between local mind and Higher Mind. Higher Mind is expansive, it's the energetic frequencies of knowing—knowing itself as well as all the localized thoughts in the thought sphere. One way to conceive of the difference between mind and Mind is that mind (with a small m) is localized in you. Your connection to local mind has been around since your childhood. Your interaction with it has always been quick and constant. Because your local mind has been supplying you with ongoing and near instantaneous thoughts ever since you can remember thinking, many people believe they are their local minds.

Higher Mind (with a capital M) is universal. It contains all knowing and is connected to everyone and everything. It is not limited by the physical constraints of your body.

Knowing the difference between Higher Mind and local mind will help you embrace Awakening. You see, local mind often works to impede the early stages of your Awakening. Most people's localized mind filters and interprets their experiences. Local mind will often purposely frame teachings like those in this book in a way that makes them sound impossible, unrealistic, or threatening. So let's talk a bit more about the nature of Higher Mind so you can have a better shot at absorbing and benefiting from this material.

Higher Mind is old. Very old. It predates your life. It even predates humanity as we know it. Higher Mind is its own consciousness, and it has its own frequency levels. Higher Mind is very, very good at making connections, organizing and laying out ideas to plan and build things, while local mind can become fixated on sorting and explaining things, often interrupting and dominating your experiences when it does.

Local mind can inhibit your connection to Higher Mind because it wants to stay in control. It can be scared. Very scared. Especially when it comes to losing control.

On the positive side, Higher Mind is creative, constructive and auspicious. On the negative side localized mind is repetitive, compulsive and destructive. As you Awaken, you'll have less of your awareness in the lower, localized levels of mind. You'll open yourself up to the higher, universal levels of mind. As you do your creativity will blossom and your work tasks will become quicker and easier to accomplish because your localized mind will not interrupt as much and you'll receive more of the higher levels of information universal Higher Mind carries.

Now here's the kicker. You are not your mind. Your mind isn't even yours.

Ask yourself the question, "Who am I?"

But before you answer, ask yourself another question.

"Who just asked, 'Who am I?'"

Your answer to the second question gives you a better understanding of your true nature and the role Higher Mind plays in the realm of your experience. You're the asker of the question. And what is doing the asking isn't your local mind, it's your consciousness. You are a consciousness.

You are a consciousness that is in relation to a local mind that allows it to interface and better understand the "reality" of the energetic density being experienced. Higher Mind is the external emanation of the thought sphere that can locally reside in you to interface between your consciousness and the stimuli you perceive from the energetic density around you, that is, all the physical stuff that makes up the 3D world we live in.

Descartes had it all confused. It's not "I think, therefore I am." It's simply "I Am."

I Am the consciousness that has awareness. A part of what I Am is aware of myself being aware, but everything after the "I Am" part of that sentence is superfluous. Descartes could have just as easily said, "I cook, therefore I am." And that would have been just as true.

Because local mind is afraid of losing control—of not being able to run your life—it will constantly feed you doubt. It will always want "proof." And even though we've all had very real experiences of extraordinary connections to Source in those moments when our Kundalini was elevated, local mind will move the goalposts and then demand an explanation, or corroboration, or the approval of some external "expert" before it will begrudgingly consider believing that a 5D experience is "real." Being aware of local mind's desperate attempts to maintain control, which manifest as doubt and thoughts of disbelief, will go a long way toward opening space within you for Awakening to blossom.

A big part of allowing your Awakening to manifest is embracing the reality that you are a consciousness. Or a soul. Or a self-aware aspect of God. Or whatever you choose to call your essence that does not diminish your magnificence.

Here are some Zen koan-like statements to help you appreciate your true essence.

Mind is not mine.

Thoughts are not mine.

Body is not mine.

There is thinking, but no thinker.

There is seeing, but no seer.

There is speaking, but no speaker.

There is doing, but no doer.

Contemplating these statements is a great beginning to accepting you are more than your physicality—more than the filters of your local mind that your consciousness uses to bridge itself to the physical realm.

Well, if you are not those things, then what are you? Consider this statement:

I am consciousness, existence, bliss.

The first part of this statement may sound familiar to you. In the Western Bible, when God was asked who he was, he replied, "I Am That I Am."

Your consciousness simply is. It doesn't need to do any thinking to prove that it is. Many people in the New Age movement understand this. You'll see lots of New Agers referring to the higher aspects of themselves as "My I Am Presence."

And because your I Am Presence is the God spark of creation itself, whatever it focuses on, it becomes. The meditative mantra presented earlier explains the creative power your consciousness possesses when you choose to focus it.

I Am That

This mantra is realization that what you focus on is what you become. Your focus, quite literally, puts you into a state of Oneness with the object of your attention. And in being that Oneness, you adopt the attributes of it. From a soul perspective, you are not those attributes. But in the third density, you may as well be. The stories you tell becomes the dictionary defining you. It becomes the mechanism by which you create your experiential reality.

This is why local mind works so hard to tell you certain stories over and over. It's how it keeps control of your life, right down to the very nature of what you do and how you see yourself. Freeing yourself from the tyranny of the lower levels of local mind expands you to understand you are in Oneness with All That Is. You are not just the limited oneness of being whatever story about yourself your local mind is telling at the moment. You are not whatever limited aspect of creation your local mind is aligning itself with to ease its fears.

Ramtha, another great being from whom I had the honor of learning, once drew a large circle on the whiteboard. He told us this represented creation. In the center he put a tiny dot, which represented ourselves. He then drew a line from that tiny dot to the edge of the circle. He told us this is the area of creation that we've mastered. The whole rest of the circle was the parts of creation that were not yet known by us. Then he shocked us all by telling us the line showing what we've mastered is misery.

We're masters of misery!

I've since come to learn that anything fully experienced turns into bliss. If I can allow and express all the emotions evoked by any experience to completely move through me, I will move into a state of bliss. If I suppress any part of the wisdom to be gained by having a complete emotional expression, I'll unconsciously stay stuck in a connection with that experience, rather than be complete and return to the essence of my being—bliss.

You see, a fundamental aspect of creation is the energy of joy. Joy, love and gratitude are more than just emotions. They are energies that creation itself is rooted in. They're sort of the background frequency that glues creation together. The mechanism of creation articulates such that when the attraction to an area of focus is completed by allowing and expressing the emotions evoked from the focus of that experience to fully express, we return to our natural state of existence. It's a state of bliss. It's the natural state consciousness finds itself in when it is free from the energetic attachment created by failing to complete an emotional experience.

Japa - A Fun Exercise to Help Embody Your True Nature

Japa is a Sanskrit word for the meditative repetition of a mantra or Divine name. You can use it to help free yourself from the programming that you are your mind. Here's how.

Every seven minutes or so, our minds take a break. It's almost like they go quiet and hit a reset button. During these times, our unconscious becomes more prevalent and we're more open to deep reprogramming.

For this japa, I recommend you engage both your body and your mind. You'll be repeating a mantra spoken aloud. And if you're a physical person, I recommend you dance. You can do it just to the rhythm of your own chanting, or with music. If you do use music, please choose something without lyrics that is upbeat and makes you feel good. Play it softly in the background, as you'll want your focus to be on your words, not on the feel of the music. And if you are physically unable to move or dance much, just sway, tap your toes, or do whatever your body is comfortable with.

Start the process by invoking your Divine. Whether you feel its presence or not, invite your Divine to be with you and imagine it is so. Then speak these koans nine or more times to set the stage for your Higher Mind to comprehend the reprogramming you'll be undergoing:

Mind is not mine

Thoughts are not mine

Body is not mine

There is thinking, but no thinker

There is seeing, but no seer

There is speaking, but no speaker

There is doing, but no doer

After speaking aloud these koans, start your music if you're using any and begin to repeat aloud over and over:

I Am consciousness, existence, bliss.

Keep chanting aloud for seven-plus minutes. Remember to go longer than just seven minutes, because you want to be actively chanting and moving during the time the pause comes up in your mind's cycle. Try setting a timer or using the length of your music playlist to keep time. You want to keep your focus on the words you're chanting not how much time you've been at it.

And as you chant, do your best to really focus on the words. The more attention you apply to the words when your mind pauses, the more deeply you'll embed your new operating code into your unconscious.

After the allotted time, lie down and be still for five minutes or so. Hold the image of golden light flooding into you directly from Source. Just relax and breathe while holding an attitude of gratitude. Then if you can, be outside and notice your connection to the environment. You will have just taken a conscious step toward your new approach to being.

Feel free to do this japa as often as you find joy in it. Once is sufficient to plant the seed. After that, it will be a matter of how aware you stay when you're expressing or defining yourself as your local mind. Awareness is key. Keep an eye out for when you speak or act like you're a mind, rather than a consciousness. Over time your entire demeanor—thoughts and actions included—will shift to a more Source-connected version of yourself.

Thoughts are an Environment Unto Themselves

Have you ever had a thought in your head just rattle around over and over and over? Sometimes it can be nice, like a catchy line from a song—at least until several days have passed and you're bored sick of it. Other times those thoughts can be quite harsh. I've asked nearly every person I've worked with if they've ever had a negative statement run over and over in their minds. You know, that thought of regret that I should have said something different, or the one of self-degradation, "I can't believe I did that. I'm so stupid. I should have done …"

Universally, everyone answers they've had those kinds of thoughts. The fact that negative, repetitive self-talk exists in all of us, is proof to me that thoughts are not ours. If thoughts were truly our own, then some people would not have experienced such negative self talk. This is why I'm ok with the understanding that thoughts are external. They exist outside of you. You are not "having" them. They are simply passing through you.

So where do thoughts come from? Let's just call it the "thought sphere." The good news is that when you're conscious of this, you can actually download information freely from the thought sphere. It's a wonderful boon to be able to simply ask to know what you need to know when you need to know it, and then have Higher Mind provide that information intuitively to you on demand. We'll speak more about how to do this in the second book of this series.

Now I'd like to address a less positive outcome that can result from the externality of thoughts. Once while I had the honor of sitting at the feet of Sri Bhagavan, he told the story of a sage who came to visit him. When they met, Bhagavan asked him how his trip was. The sage confessed he was troubled. He'd been having murderous thoughts all afternoon and it was quite upsetting to him. Bhagavan asked him where did he stop to eat lunch? When the sage told him, Bhagavan said, "Oh, a teenage boy killed his girlfriend under that tree. You picked up his murderous thoughts there."

Even though he was wise, the sage did not yet have the awareness that thoughts are external. He did not know that you pass through thoughts, or that thoughts can pass through you. If you're not aware of this, then you have little choice as to whether or not a thought stays with you. Awareness is the tool that frees you from repetitive thoughts. Once you look at a thought from the point of view of your consciousness, you're free from it. The thought is not yours. It's just something in the environment where your local mind is at that moment.

Once the thought has been acknowledged as not yours, its attachment to you will lessen. And thoughts you deem as "negative" will then only stay with you if there's blocked emotional energy attracting it. When you get to step 2 later in this book, you'll know how to complete your blocked emotions and free yourself from attracting and holding on to thoughts you no longer desire.

This is why it's so important to be aware of the stories you tell, especially about yourself. By speaking the words of a thought, you can attach yourself to it. And the more you speak them, the more you're attached. After a while, it won't just be your "story." You'll identify with it so much, it will be your life, your identity. This process is what I'm talking about when I say local mind wants to be in control. It wants to be the arbiter of who you are. And you're complicit in this by habitually telling what you call your story over and over again.

It really doesn't matter what happened to you. Or even what your mind says you "learned" from the experience. Your body doesn't know the difference between something real or imagined. Your body gives you the same visceral reaction whether it's a real-life event or if you're watching it happen in a movie. So if you choose to remember something over and over by continuing to tell the story of it, your body will react to it as if was happening in real time. In a sense, you'll become addicted to the peptides your body releases in reaction to the emotions you reacted with from that event. Talk about getting hooked on a lousy drug, eh?

Because local mind can be polarized by fear, it will seek out thoughts from the thought sphere to confirm its bias and keep you afraid. In its effort to "protect" you, it actually imprisons you. The more you subscribe to the notion that you are anything less than your consciousness, the more your life becomes limited. You stop growing. You become an amalgam of your stories. "This happened to me, so I'm this way." You will call your well-worn mental tracks "habits" or "my personality."

Your story, especially if you tell it over and over, is an anchor. Be aware of what you choose to talk about. If an event already happened, why are you telling it again? The day before writing this passage, a relative dropped by after what he described as an uncomfortable drive. He complained about how long it took, how much traffic there was, and how annoyed he was by all this. As I listened, I couldn't help but feel sad. If that experience was so terrible, why was he choosing to repeat it? He was now sitting with me in a beautiful courtyard. Why was he still on the road suffering through traffic?

I'm not sharing this to criticize him or to disparage mind. Mind is great when it's an ally. Writing this book was possible because mind worked to identify the concepts and organize them. Mind builds things, it helps discover things. When in a state of flow, mind is super cool! But in order to allow Awakening energies to blossom within us, we must first quiet our local minds by focusing on and embracing that we are first and foremost, a consciousness. As we Awaken, it's very important to be aware of our thoughts and words. Do you really want to filter out the awareness and wisdom of experience by having your local mind continually curate it?

As you Awaken, it's important to bring awareness to how frequently your thoughts interrupt an experience and then do your best to bring your attention back to that experience. Try it when you brush your teeth. Can you spend even a mere 30 seconds just noticing the feel of each brushstroke in your mouth?

After an experience, are you quick to tell people about it, rehashing what you've already experienced through the filter of your local mind, or do you remain quiet and embrace your next experience?

And when you do relate your experience to someone, what story do you tell them? Do you tell the story of victimhood? "Oh I suffered through traffic!" Or do you want to create new possibilities by telling a story of becoming? Consider thinking of your words as prayers, or spells you are casting. Try being aware of when you curse yourself by speaking forth a terrible outcome before you've even had an experience. Play the game of trying to turn your words into prayers of manifestation. You know, like in the book *The Secret* and all that's been revealed about manifestation. Those teachings are true. Consider speaking aloud the outcomes you desire and remaining quiet about everything else. Wouldn't that be an adventure!

On a recent vacation while hiking through cenotes near Cancun, my wife suddenly announced, "Everything of mine always comes back to me. I'm excited that the fitness tracker that's not now in my new wristband is coming back to me."

Sure enough, when we emerged from the caves about two hours later, her daughter saw a glint of light from under a bush by the trail. When she investigated, it was my wife's fitness tracker. Rather than telling a story about something she lost, she told a story of what she finds. And sure enough, she found what she desired.

Realize that whatever story you tell, it's the story of what you are being. So what are you choosing? Are you telling the story of what you're becoming? Or are you telling the story of what you've been? By speaking only of your magnificence with gratitude, you may lose your sense of identity, of who you were. And considering that most of us have only been masters of misery, is this really a bad thing?

If you allow Source to work its benevolent magic (by clearing out your emotional blockages as we'll discuss in step 2), you'll find that giving voice to thoughts only when they're uplifting and affirm your desires will make you a whole lot happier!

Receive Awakening

I was blessed (literally and figuratively).

Awakening was given to me by great beings and spiritual teachers whose missions on Earth were to uplift humanity at this auspicious time. Until recently, that was how it was done. Masters passed it down to students. Throughout most of recorded history, there were only a handful of Awakened people on Earth at any one time. And whenever a fully enlightened soul showed up, the impact was so profound that a great religion usually ended up forming around that person's teaching. At this time, Earth has moved into a new energetic frequency and everyone is now able to receive Awakening.

In the decades leading up to the birth of the Golden Age in 2012, many "advanced" souls came to the planet to assist in our transition. Many traditions began to pass on Awakening to all who were ready to receive it. I was involved in the Oneness movement founded by Sri Amma and Sri Bhagavan in India. Their goal was to bring 144,000 people from around the world into Awakening. And then to instill in them the ability to Awaken others. My Sacred Higher Self tells me that between their efforts and those of many other teachers all across the globe, tens of millions of people on Earth are currently Awakened. And many of us have embodied the ability to transfer it.

Through their efforts, the energetic field of Awakening has been established on Earth. This means that everyone will soon experience beginning levels of Awakening naturally, simply by being around others who carry these energies. However, why wait for it to take hold and slowly progress in your life. You're reading this book because you want to make conscious contact with your Higher Self. And I'm writing it because I want to help you do so—quickly.

Below I've outlined three simple ways you can receive and amplify your Awakening. We're able to take advantage of the Ascension energies rooted on the planet by the teachers and great beings who've laid the groundwork in decades past. Because Awakening is firmly rooted on the planet, you're going to receive it simply by choosing to stay alive on the planet at this time. If you'd like to actively take part in receiving Awakening, start by acknowledging that you've already embodied the beginning levels of Awakening in your life. You're reading this book because you are attracted to Ascending, and that means Awakening has already come to you at least a little. Please join me in choosing to self-direct your Ascension by amplifying the Awakening energies within you. Here are three ways of the many ways you can do so.

Ask Source Directly to Give Awakening to You

Awakening was a gift given to me by a highly evolved being who chose to be in a physical body for this purpose. But we're now past the time of having to go through intermediaries to receive the benevolence of the Divine. You can ask Source directly to give Awakening to you. This ability is the fruit of the labors of many who have come before us to plow the road, so to speak, so that everyone can now travel down it with ease.

Now by "asking" I don't really mean you have to ask. Awakening is coming to everyone who chooses to be incarnate on Earth at this time. It's in the energy field, so it's happening automatically. By asking, I mean allowing yourself to receive these energies in an accelerated manner. This is done by "praying" for it. And by praying, I don't mean in the traditional sense of how most of us were taught to pray.

Most people think of prayer as asking God for a boon or blessing. We need a new blueprint for prayer now that we're Ascending into 5D energies. Here's what I've learned about how to pray in a manner that yields results.

First, you don't ever "ask" for anything. Asking puts you in a dynamic that unconsciously assumes that you, the asker, do not have what you seek. It creates the false notion of lack, fixing your consciousness in a place and time where what you desire does not exist. In 5D, it ALL already exists. Thus when you engage in asking, you're pulling your consciousness out of the abundance of all that is into a 3D timeline of lack.

Another unconscious dynamic of asking as part of your prayer is that it separates you from God. It puts you in a place where you're not already in the Kingdom of Heaven with all the riches that await you. Worse still, it creates a hierarchy where you, at the lower end of things, don't have, and God, at the higher end, does. As such, you have to ask to receive it. In 5D you're on equal footing with God. She's still the creator of ALL THAT IS, but you're a cocreator within the framework of creation. The Ascension of Earth means the planet is already moving into 5D. Your ticket to enter is simply to step into the new energies. So you don't ask when you pray.

Envision you already have it and give gratitude for having received such a bounty.

That's the new rules of prayer for 5D. Engage all your senses to see, feel, hear, taste and touch what you desire as if you already have it. Use your imagination to create scenes in which you experience what it's like to have the object of your desire. The more "real" you can make your imagining, the closer you come to flipping into the timeline where you already have it.

You want that new car? See it. The sporty red one with the top down. Feel the wind in your hair. Smell the new car smell as it mingles with the crisp, salty air on a spring day as you're driving down the coastal highway. Make imagination of your manifestation as real as possible by fleshing out the details and engaging all your senses.

Then power your visualization with a high vibration emotion. Gratitude, love and joy are some of the highest-frequency vibrations that exist. So as you engage your senses to feel into your creation, feel gratitude that you've already received it. Feel love for how wonderful it feels to have already received that which you are creating through your imaginings. Feel the exhilaration of how your new car is hugging the curves of the road with each turn you take in your imagination.

Once you've done this, you're done. If you've done it correctly, there's no need to do it again—other than it feels good to let your consciousness float back into the expansiveness of creation and the joy you're supplying to empower it. Don't be like a kid on a long drive and continually ask, "Are we there yet?" When you board a flight for a cross-country journey, do you relax in your seat until you arrive or do you go knock on the cockpit door and yell for the pilot to hurry up? Which of these actions better embodies the joyful frequency that you already have what you desire?

As a side note, group prayers are stronger, and prayers empowered by a group consciousness are even stronger still. There will be more explanation about this in the third book of this series, *My Ascension Handbook – Level III*.

When you pray, know that you're being heard. There may be a lag in 3D time and space because Spirit is having to arrange the physical aspects of this density to put the right people and events in place. But it is being done.

And since prayer is a sacred act, treat it that way. Do whatever rituals you do to get into a sacred space before praying. Some people take baths because they want to be clean for their God. I like to keep my house neat because I view God as a guest in my life and I want my space to be inviting to him. Some people have altars. Some burn fragrant herbs or incense. Some make offerings. Some kneel. There's no one correct 3D spell or movements that make prayer sacred. It's up to you and how you choose to honor your relationship with the Divine. I've found that making the effort to be sacred when I pray engages my subconscious and my soul on a deeper level and I get better results.

There you have it. Ask your Divine to give your Awakening. Do it by seeing, hearing, tasting, smelling, feeling and imagining yourself having the kinds of Awakened experiences I described earlier in this chapter—especially a quiet mind and a gap between the experience you are having and when your mind kicks in to "explain" the experience to you. And have as much joy and gratitude as you can during your prayer. After you pray, do your best to allow it to come to you. Remember that what intending was to manifestation in 3D, allowing is to manifestation in 5D.

In case you're wondering why I'm continually comparing 3D to 5D, while skipping over 4D, here's your answer. 4D is a transitional phase between 3D and 5D. It is that it is a training ground for 5D. Manifestation is quicker in 4D, but not yet instantaneous.

Nearly everyone living in 3D has a backlog of mostly negative unconscious beliefs. If we had the ability to instantly manifest, most of us would unknowingly create a shit show. Sure, you may be pretty clear you want that pretty pony for your daughter's tenth birthday, but your unconscious may have attached beliefs like it's a lot of hard work to care for a pony, or that they are dirty animals that muck things up, or that hay and a barn stall will cost an arm and a leg. These unconscious beliefs attached to the joy of having a pony probably won't surface until you actually manifest the pony. And then their unexpected nature can blindside you. That's why your prayers may take some time before they are answered as you transition into 5D. It's necessary for you to clear the unconscious energies you're holding that have limited your experience to 3D in the first place. That's what the space in 4D provides.

As you invite in 5D energies and practice the method of prayer I've outlined, you may find all kinds of resistances arise within you. Unconscious beliefs such as I can never have that. I don't deserve it. Or it's a bad thing to want that so I shouldn't ask for it. The method of prayer outlined above builds a place for all these resistances to surface. I call them "charges." And believe you me, when you practice this method of prayer, all kinds of charges will surface. Welcome them!

Your charges arising are a good thing. It's why we have the transitional fourth density. Your charges need to be brought to consciousness so they can be transformed. Ascension depends on you clearing all the lower, denser unconscious energies keeping you rooted in 3D. You simply cannot vibrate at lighter 5D frequencies if you're still holding heavier 3D energies. That's what the transition space of 4D allows. It lets you have one leg in 3D while you practice what's coming for you to enjoy in 5D. We'll speak more about identifying and clearing charges in step 2 of this book, as well as offering another system for clearing charges that is really helpful for ongoing maintenance in the second book of this series. For now, just notice your charges should they arise as you pray. Awareness is the first step to clearing. And it's an important one.

One last note about 5D prayer before moving on to the second way you can receive Awakening. I would be remiss to offer you these teachings about prayer without teaching you the most powerful prayer ever!

Thank you, more please.

You know that high vibration of gratitude we just discussed? And remember how I told you allowing is the new intent when it comes to 5D manifesting? This prayer does both. Say it often.

Anytime anything comes your way that makes you happy, say it.

Thank you, more please.

While we're in the transition zone of 4D, this simple prayer acknowledges that what you prefer is coming to you, even if it is just a little bit to start. I asked a mother I was helping the other day how she would feel if her two-year-old said to her, "Thank you, more please." She said she'd melt and of course, give her child more. So when the Divine hears you say it, what do you think it will do? Of course, it sends you more. Your Source will direct more of the frequency of abundant benevolence toward you—as much as you allow yourself to receive.

Remember that it's OK to start little. You want $10,000 and you find a dime on the street. What do you say?

Thank you, more please.

Though tiny, this powerful prayer lets the universe know you're ready to receive whatever it can give. And since the universe is an expression of God's love, you know what's going to happen. The universe is going to give you more.

Ideally, the Divine would give everything to you all the time. But because we have free will, and because here in 3D most of us used our free will to unconsciously create all kinds of beliefs and emotional blockages that prevent us from receiving, only small dribs and drabs can trickle through. Saying, "Thank you, more please" literally opens us up to receiving more. So that's what comes. It's a great prayer. Please make it your go-to prayer, and say it many, many times during your day.

Raise your Kundalini with Breath Work

The energetic field of Awakening is already rooted on Earth. Most people are already experiencing the beginning stages of Awakening. That's why saying the "Thank you, more please" prayer can now be so powerful. Some children are now even being born fully Awakened, which will strengthen Earth's Awakening field all the more. But left to its own devices, the full transition to everyone on the planet being Awakened will take about four hundred years. And if you're reading this book, you certainly don't want to wait that long while external charges burn themselves off and all the nastiness of societal institutions are slowly exposed and ameliorated.

As you do your internal work, you'll receive Awakening quicker and stronger. It's sort of like how a farmer plows the ground and fertilizes the soil before planting. Breath work prepares your body to hold better alignment with Awakening energies. Here are two ancient practices that will really prepare for Awakening to ramp up in a big way within you: Chakra Dhyana and Ananda Mandala meditation.

The Chakra Dhyana

Much has been written on Chakra Dhyana. Please consider doing more research if you'd like to learn more. Only the basics are included here—enough information to practice it so you can receive the benefits of doing it. The Chakra Dhyana is a meditation that uses your breath to focus on and balance each of your seven major chakras (i.e., energy centers in your body). The practice combines a physical posture, with breath, sound and a mental focus, integrating all parts of your physical being to better balance you and allow your body to receive more of the transformative Awakening energies.

Before you get overwhelmed trying to understand all the parts of a Chakra Dhyana, please give a moment of gratitude that several beautiful souls have produced free videos allowing you to easily follow along as they guide you through this practice. I've written as concise a description as I can. If you're drawn to practicing Chakra Dhyana, please read through this section to familiarize yourself with the process, then use the video links at the end of this section to dive in.

In the centerline of this image, you can see where your seven main chakras are located. To the left is the Sanskrit name for each of them. On the right is the root sound associated with each one. And the inset photos on the far right show the hand posture (mudra) to hold while focusing on the corresponding chakras.

Posture

Sit up with your spine straight. You can be cross-legged or in a chair, but don't lie down. As long as you keep your spine as straight as you can, sit comfortably.

There are three hand gestures you'll use. These amplify and cycle the energy channels (nadis) for the chakra you're focusing on. Rest your hands on your thighs, palms up. For the lower three chakras, touch your forefingers to the tip of your thumb. For the next two chakras in your heart and throat area, touch your forefingers to the middle joint of your thumb. For the upper chakras in your third eye and crown areas, hold your forefingers to the joint at the base of your thumb.

Focus

Each chakra is located in an area of your body. As Chakra Dhyana progresses, you'll be asked to focus on these areas. Please refer to the image above to help you visualize where each chakra resides.

Your first chakra, sometimes called your root chakra, sits at the base of your spine.

Your second chakra is located just above your genitals.

Your third chakra can be located anywhere from just behind your navel up to your solar plexus (belly button to breastbone).

Your fourth chakra, sometimes called your heart chakra, rests with your heart.

Your fifth chakra is located in your throat.

Your sixth chakra, sometimes called your third eye, is in your forehead at the point between and behind your eyes.

Your seventh chakra, sometimes called your crown chakra, is just above your head.

Each of these chakras also has a color they emanate. During Chakra Dhyana, when you're asked to bring your focus to a certain chakra, it will be helpful to visualize where it is in your body and see or imagine its color.

The root chakra is pure red.

The second chakra is orange.

The third chakra is yellow.

The heart chakra is green.

The throat chakra is blue. Often a lighter or turquoise/teal blue.

The third eye chakra is purple indigo.

The crown chakra is violet or white.

As you focus on each chakra, you can imagine a ball or wheel of that color spinning in the appropriate place in your body.

Sound

In addition to each chakra having a Sanskrit name, there's a seed sound for each one. These sounds (called beej in Hindi) carry the vibrational frequency of each chakra. Saying it while focusing on that chakra amplifies your connection to it. Don't worry about how to pronounce them correctly. The pronunciation is included as part of a chant in the videos linked to below.

The name of the root chakra is muladhara. Its sound is lang.

The name of the second chakra is svadhisthana. Its sound is vang.

The name of the third root chakra is manipura. Its sound is rang.

The name of the heart chakra is anahata. Its sound is yang.

The name of the throat chakra is vishuddhi. Its sound is hang.

The name of the third eye chakra is agnya. Its sound is aum.

The name of the crown chakra is sahasrara. Its sound is ogum satyam om.

Guided Chakra Dhyana Meditations

These guided Chakra Dhyana meditations are posted on YouTube.

Here is a beautiful and brief (15-minute) guided Chakra Dhyana by Angelika. You can find her YouTube Channel by searching for *Angelika – Topic*, or following this link: https://youtube.com/channel/UCZ3Uae-ILZUlGtj81tXhG8A

You can find the introductory explanation by searching on YouTube for *Chakra Dhyanna Intro Talk*, or by following this link: https://youtu.be/ToT0gYBhpo4

You can find her full guided Chakra Dhyana meditation by searching on YouTube for *Chakra Dhyanna* or by following this link: https://youtu.be/LZtf30cECpk

(Please note that when you search for Angelika's meditations on YouTube, she spells Chakra Dhyana with two *n*'s: Chakra Dhyanna.)

And here is Ananda Giri's forty-minute guided Chakra Dhyana. You can find it on YouTube by searching for *Ananda Giri – The Oneness Chakra Meditation*, or by following this link: https://youtu.be/2jbLyITT0Wo

Other Benefits of the Chakra Dhyana

Besides preparing your body to receive Awakening to the fullest extent you can, doing Chakra Dhyana provides a whole host of other health benefits:

- It helps heal hurts, removes fear, anxiety, tension, stress, insecurities and lust.

- It fills you with positive energies and vibrations in the body, mind and heart.

- It enables a flowering of your heart.

- It results in increased focus and concentration.

- It helps in goal setting.

- It can result in mystical experiences.

The Chakra Dhyana is easier to do compared to Ananda Mandala meditation, and can effectively be done on your own. The Ananda Mandala meditation is more intense. It will raise your Kundalini higher, quicker. But you may not hold it in that higher state for as long afterward. Please read about Ananda Mandala meditation before choosing to do one, or both, of the techniques suggested.

The Ananda Mandala Meditation

Ananda Mandala means "bliss circle." It is a practice that uses a more aggressive breathing technique, similar to a "breath of fire," to put you in a very high state of elevated Kundalini flow very quickly. Ananda Mandala meditation is most effective when done in a group. It can also be used to clear negative trapped emotions. And it feels great to do it. Don't be surprised when the people you're doing it with break out into uncontrolled fits of laughter while practicing it.

However, there are a couple of contraindications to practicing Ananda Mandala meditation. Do not do it if you are pregnant, if you have a heart condition or have recently had surgery. And should the experience become too much for you at any point, just return to normal breathing. Simply being in a group and holding hands with others doing the Ananda Mandala meditation will raise your Kundalini. Or consider practicing Chakra Dhyana until you're more used to your Kundalini being in such a peak state.

Begin by sitting and then blowing your nose. Keep a tissue handy as you'll likely need it again. Sit in a circle, gently holding hands. Everyone should have their thumbs pointing left to keep the energy flowing between you steady. You'll be guided to breathe in on the count of one, and out on two. Breathe through your nose if you can, as most of your nadis terminate their connection there. Your exhale should be a sharp, forceful motion from your diaphragm, quickly pushing out the air in your lungs. Your inhale will come naturally by simply relaxing your diaphragm, allowing your belly to move outward.

The one-two count of breaths will become increasingly quicker. Eventually you will inhale and hold your breath, focusing on the chakra the guide directs you to. Then you will exhale, hold your breath and focus on your crown chakra. You won't be chanting the names of the chakras like you do in Chakra Dhyana.

When you're finished, return to normal breathing while focusing on your crown. Then lay down in shavasana (the corpse yoga pose) to integrate and recuperate.

Guided Ananda Mandala Meditations

These guided Ananda Mandala meditation practices have been graciously posted on YouTube.

Here is a beautiful and brief (22-minute) guided Ananda Mandala meditation by Angelika. You can find her YouTube Channel by searching for "Angelika – Topic," or following this link: https://youtube.com/channel/UCZ3Uae-ILZUlGtj81tXhG8A

Angelika offers these videos for the Ananda Mandala meditation:

Introductory Explanation • Search on YouTube for "Ananda Mandala Intro Talk," or follow this link: https://youtu.be/LjZJQiFpO5k

Guided Meditation • Search on YouTube for "Ananda Mandala meditation," or follow this link: https://youtu.be/LZtf30cECpk

And here is Ananda Giri's forty-four-minute guided Ananda Mandala meditation that includes time to rest and recover afterward. You can find it on YouTube by searching for "Ananda Mandala – Kundalini Breath Technique," or by following this link: https://youtu.be/aPY2N_HFYr8

Please know I am not affiliated with any of the people I've listed links for in this chapter. I've provided them to make your practice of these processes easier. However, if you understand the flow of abundance, you may wish to purchase a CD from Angelika as a thank you. Here's the link to her sales page: https://angelikahealingmusic.com/music/

You can simply type in "Ananda Giri" on Amazon if you'd like to see a display of his teachings and music you can purchase.

Find Someone Who is Awakened and Ask Them to Bless You with It

I was blessed in that Awakening, along with the ability to transfer Awakening, was given to me. Oneness University was founded by Sri Amma/Bhagavan to help shepherd in the Golden Age. The Oneness movement they spearheaded gave Awakening to hundreds of thousands of people across the globe. Many of us were initiated to pass Awakening along to others. And the Oneness movement was only one of many movements, schools and teachers who helped ground Awakening energies into Gaia's planetary grid. Now it's fixed into place and slowly, but surely, nearly everyone incarnate on Earth will Awaken.

However, this process of everyone fully Awakening will take several generations, making the process of Ascension for everyone on the planet even longer. You don't need to be too observant of the state of the world to know there're many, many terrible things that have been done and must be undone for the Golden Age to fully set in. That's why I'm writing this series of Ascension Handbooks, and why I've included this section of the book. The entire process, both Awakening and Ascension, can be sped up and completed in our lifetime. Giving and receiving Awakening is a quick way of doing so.

I've produced a quick video transmitting Awakening. It's only eight minutes long and the first three minutes of it is an explanation. You can simply skip ahead to the transmission after you've seen it once. You can find it on my YouTube Channel by searching for "Becoming Awesome," or following this link: https://youtube.com/@PeterDeBen

Look for the video titled "Receive Awakening" or follow this link: https://youtu.be/qjl3QI4ECf4

I will also be hosting eight to ten larger live-streamed Q&A sessions a year that will include group meditations and transmissions for Awakening and God-realization. These sessions will be given on a donation basis, so don't worry about what it costs. Just join in and if you're moved with gratitude, you can follow up with a financial gift. You'll be able to find out about these sessions on my website by typing becomingawesome.one into your browser address bar. Then look under the classes/events tab. Or follow this link for a complete schedule and information on how to register: https://becomingawesomeone.com/events/

I will also be offering weekend classes to take you through the processes described in this book. Clearings, meditations and transmissions are much stronger when done in groups along with people already holding the energies you are hoping to receive. Use the Classes/Events link provided in the previous paragraph to find out when the classes are taking place and how you can enroll.

And please know I am not the only person able to transmit Awakening to you. There are hundreds of thousands of others who have been initiated by Oneness University who can do so. And there are people from numerous other traditions who can provide this to you as well. Ask around among people you know who seem calmer and more present. When you find someone, check in with your intuition to see if their energy field is clear or if there're other things going on with them that you don't want to receive.

And even if the person you find doesn't know "how to transmit" Awakening, it's really not hard to do once you are Awakened. It's simple.

1. Invoke the presence of Source

2. Connect into the field of Oneness

3. Link your consciousness with the person you are transmitting to

4. Ask your Divine to step up and make the transmission of what you have

5. Step aside and let your Divine do the rest

6. End the transmission with gratitude

Fully Awakening May Take Some Time

Though I have seen people fully Awaken after receiving a single transmission of Awakening energy, for most people it takes some time for the seeds of Awakening to blossom once they are planted. So don't go beating yourself up if things aren't moving as quickly as you'd like. Usually it's a sign that you still have charges to clear, which is the topic the next chapter will address. Use your impatience as a tool to guide you to the blockages still holding you back.

Remember, your body can only move so quickly as far as the neurobiological shift Awakening requires. Give yourself plenty of time to rest and relax. Continue practicing either Chakra Dhyana or Ananda Mandala meditation and continue receiving Awakening energies from your Divine or another person. Remember the prayer *Thank you, more please* to celebrate your progress as you notice what may seem like small changes occurring in and around you. The more you are aware of and allow the changes to take place, the more they will happen—and they'll be quicker too.

Practicing awareness is a powerful way to let Awakening energies fully transform you. Be as mindful as you can of what is taking place in your experience. What are you seeing, smelling, hearing, tasting, and touching? Do not keep feeding your mind. It's not about what you think. Just notice you're having a thought and then bring your focus back to your experience. Do this as often as you become aware that you're back in the thought sphere bouncing around an expression of your being as ideas and memories.

As best you can, stop telling stories. It doesn't serve you to know why everything around you is happening. It's just a big distraction local mind uses to make you think you're on top of things. When in reality, it's local mind that is on top, feeding you thought after thought of explanation or interrupting an experience by asking *why* it's happening. Pay more attention to how you feel, rather than why something is or isn't taking place in a certain way.

Basically, once you have received Awakening, you need to start acting like it for Awakening to really take hold and transform you. Awareness is the first step to doing this. Be aware of how your local mind acts to hold you back. Consider that your mind is like a freight train that's been going down the tracks at one hundred miles per hour your whole life. Suddenly, you're Awakened and it's like the clutch has been pulled and you've shifted into neutral. Your mind is still speeding along, but there's no longer an engine driving it. Your local mind will try to maintain control and tell you nothing has really changed. It's up to you to practice awareness. Notice the changes. Practice focusing on them instead of your repeating thoughts, memories and book-learned explanations of what's taking place. As often as you can, move your awareness back to your senses and just be present. The freight train will eventually slow down.

Now please don't construe from this book that mind is your enemy. Mind is just doing what it's done for a long time. And it will be uncomfortable when you start doing things differently. It will likely tell you that the changes you're making aren't working. That you're wasting your time. That everything in this book is full of crap.

I like to use the analogy of a fussy grandmother. She's in the living room watching TV. When you walk in, she starts at you. "You need a haircut. Are you really going out looking that way? You've got a stain on your clothes. Are you still dating that terrible guy? I don't like him …"

Because she's your Grams, you love her. She raised you. But now all she can do is go on and on about negative things. What can you do? I say, "Thank you, Grams. I love you so much. I really have to go now. Bye."

I notice when my mind is playing out the fussy grandmother role. I thank it and I move on. Awareness is the first step.

And just like your local mind can provide you with endless internal negative chatter, TV and mass media, especially the news, are designed to provide you with endless external negative chatter. If you haven't already done so, please consider turning off and tuning out the news, including the alternative news sources that are supposedly giving you the hidden truth.

News is bought and paid for by entities that wish to maintain power in 3D. It's purposefully designed to repeat negativity so you'll believe the sorry state of the world is normal. If you want to start living in 5D, letting go of the 3D storytelling provided by news is an important step.

And although well-meaning, alternative news providers don't really help free you from 3D either. They just change the narrative of the stories trying to occupy your consciousness. They speak about hidden good people coming to save us once enough people learn the truth.

Besides being disempowering by promoting the narrative of someone outside yourself being your liberator, alternative news gives rise to what I call "disasterbation." It's created a whole class of people who believe they're in the know and are on a mission to tell you about all the terrible ways you're being poisoned and controlled. You've probably seen people get together and play the game of sharing how horrible so and so is because of this and that going on behind our backs.

The end result of their disasterbating is the same as what the controllers want to create—a disempowered population immersed in low-energy fear vibrations. Wouldn't you rather move your vibrations into higher energies? You don't cross over into 5D by complaining about and fighting against 3D. You leave those energies behind by focusing your awareness on 5D. How good it feels. How exciting and limitless the possibilities are there. How powerful you are in creating it by focusing on it!

The bottom line is that Awakening doesn't really do you any good if you don't use the levels of consciousness it opens up for you. Follow your intuitive impulses. If you don't rely on your intuition, what good is having it? This means being open to freedom from social norms, even when it seems uncomfortable to do so. As you Awaken it will be you and your God now calling the shots. Listen to that voice within and act on it.

I know lots of spiritually aware people at the beginning stages of Awakening who stagnate because they just don't follow the guidance they are already receiving. This book and many other wisdom teachers are offering amazing tools to help people ascend. But a lot of people seem to go out of their way to avoid embracing what's now possible. Some don't want to give up letting their mind run the show. Doing so would mean losing their "identity" and all the mental props holding up their self-image.

Some people can let go of their mind running the show, but are loathe to change habits. Usually because they'd lose the place of their ego. They'd have to let go of being right, or what they've believed has made them content. Letting go of their habits is unconsciously seen as a greater burden than doing what it takes to allow themselves to receive all they desire.

Others are simply scared. On an unconscious level, they know that Ascension means they must let go of all the low vibrational energy they're holding. And quite simply, they're afraid of their own fear. Or anger. Or emotional pain. They do their best to ignore the impulses to grow into Ascension by finding reasons why they should keep doing the same things over and over again, even though they don't produce the results they're secretly hoping for—and even more secretly believe they aren't worthy of having.

Pointing this out is not a condemnation. I'm trying to bring awareness to the state of consciousness (or unconsciousness) most of us lived in before we began our Ascension process. It really has simply been holding trapped emotional energies. Humanity is now at the point where we're going to have to begin releasing these or suffer the consequences more profoundly through our bodies expressing aging and experiencing disease. Instead, let's release these denser energies that have been unconsciously trapped in many of us.

Step 2 – Clear Emotional Blockages

Anything fully expressed turns to bliss.

Sri Bhagavan

The energy of emotions was meant to flow unhindered. It is necessary to "complete" an experience by becoming aware and physically expressing its emotional component. Emotional expression is how our half of the interaction with an external experience completes. With its completion we grow. We gain wisdom. And the energy that created the circumstance of that experience is released and flows freely to the next experience it empowers in creation.

But often we do not complete an experience. We truncate it before the emotional component is expressed. Our mind, if in control, can shut it down. You know how a person can begin to get emotional and then simply announce, "I don't want to go there." Or our bodies can freeze up. And it's not just "big" emotions that get choked off from expression. Over time blocking emotions can become habitual and even the "smallest" of emotions can shut down.

Most of us did not grow up in an environment that supported emotional release. It just wasn't safe for many of us to freely express emotions when we were children. And few of us had parents who modeled emotional release, let alone supported us when we did.

Why Fully Experiencing Emotions Is Important

Most of us live in a world where local mind rules the roost, we've created codes of honor and tenets of ethics to ostensibly guide our interactions. The problem is that these belief systems lack the wisdom of your personal experience. They're codices of other people's conclusions—many of which don't even include the wisdom of that person's emotional experiences having been completed. It's just mental beliefs piled on top of other mental beliefs.

Both you and God require emotional completion in order to grow.

Our natural state of existence is bliss. Remember who you are? Consciousness, existence, bliss.

God requires us to complete an experience in order for creation to grow. You see, as a single consciousness, God could not experience anything more than it already was. It's not like God is over in one spot and the rest of the universe is somewhere else, and God goes over to that other part of the universe to explore. No. God *is* the universe. The consciousness of the universe is God, or God is the consciousness of the universe—however you care to say it. So even though its existence is blissful, it's limited. It's only as big as God, which although it's everything, it's still limited.

This caused God to figure out how to grow. God needed input from than its singular expression of itself in order to conceive of and experience something it didn't already know. And since God was everything already, there was nothing outside itself. Thus God created a "simulation" in which parts of itself would forget they were God. It's kind of like a computer that is not connected to the Internet. It still has all the computing power it was built with, it just can't access the whole net. But unlike a computer that needs someone else to provide it input, we've been created with physical senses and other, esoteric senses, that are designed to kick in when we completely process an experience.

This is how God individuated its consciousness. And when it came to humanity, God gave those fractals of its consciousness free will. It put in place a barrier of forgetfulness so that to some degree we wouldn't be born knowing we were God. This allowed billions and billions of God-sparked consciousnesses to do their thing in whatever way they chose. It created all kinds of unknown permutations of experience. And what was previously a limited set of experiences for God to enjoy suddenly grew, and continues to grow, exponentially.

We're God's eyes and ears—the billions and billions of us on Earth and many, many more nonphysical fractals of God throughout other dimensional densities. And there are countless more in physical forms across the stars. We're the leading edge of creation. Our experiences literally fuel the expansion of God. It's super cool! We complete an experience and we grow. We complete an experience and God grows.

When emotions flow freely, so does our connection with Source. When emotions are blocked, so too is our spiritual connection. The dense energy it takes to stop an emotion from being felt internally also stops feeling from taking place externally. Our conscious contact with the Divine gets severed.

Fortunately, creation is powered by benevolence. There's a self-regulating mechanism built in to help prevent emotions from staying blocked. The blocked energy of a trapped emotion carries with it a magnetic resonance that attracts similar experiences. In this way, if you didn't complete the emotion the first time you had the experience that gave it rise, you'll have a second opportunity to complete the emotion by having another experience like it.

The problem is that if we didn't have the wherewithal to fully experience an event the first time, it's not very likely the experience will be completed the second time either. So for many of us, the emotional blockage gets bigger. And the universe compensates by providing an even bigger experience to try to break loose the trapped emotions. It could have started innocently when you were a small child who was afraid to open your closet because you forgot a half-eaten bologna sandwich in there and it was all moldy when you saw it a month later. Not fully experiencing that fear then could have caused layers and layers of additional fear-inducing experiences to be attracted to you. And these could have grown so much that as you get older, you're afraid to even go outside because it's a dirty world full of germs and disease.

Left unexpressed, blocked emotions, which I also called "charges," take a huge toll on our bodies. They are literally the cause of aging and disease. You see, blocked emotions are stored as stuck energy in our bodies. Nearly every person I've worked with to clear blocked emotions is able to pinpoint a place in their body where they feel a discomfort when they are asked to feel the emotion we're clearing. These points of discomfort are literally "dis-ease." They're seed locations that can grow into disease over time as your Kundalini is prevented from flowing through that area because the dense nature of the suppressed emotions blocks it.

And it's not just our bodies that deteriorate from unexpressed emotional energy. Our entire life circumstances are affected.

Have you ever heard someone say, "That always happens to me?"

The attractive nature of trapped emotions is what fuels similar circumstances happening to us over and over again. And just like our bodies die from the diseases created by blocked emotions, so too do our lives deteriorate from greater and greater difficulties being drawn to us to try and shake loose a lifetime of trapped emotions layered on top of each other. Some people just keep avoiding their emotional blockages until they have a devastating divorce, their career is abruptly terminated, their house burns down, they get in a debilitating car crash or some other midlife crisis or dark night of the soul shakes them loose.

So why wait until the crap hits the fan before you clear your emotional blockages? Why not take active steps to enjoy the freedom and connections clearing your emotions can give you right now? Here's a testimonial from someone who had the courage to face her blockages:

> *[The clearing we did] was a gift my soul was waiting for! To first acknowledge to myself and then feel ABANDONMENT, LOSS and NOT BEING LOVED was so difficult! I wanted to run away! I stayed and knew I was being protected! Peter, when you asked me to sit on my Divine Mother's lap, hold her hand and just let her hold me tight and kiss me, for a moment I resisted. I wanted so badly to feel*

our connection. It took me a while to let go and just be. As I continued to feel the pain in my high heart where I felt ABANDONMENT, I was so aware of continuing to hold tightly my Divine Mother's hand. When you asked me to invite ABANDONMENT in I did! I felt the congestion in my high heart begin to loosen. I went immediately to the safety of my Divine Mother's arms and held on tight. At that moment I was so conscious of my ability to transmute the pain of ABANDONMENT and open my heart and receive My Divine Mother's LOVE, filling up my high heart. Consciously inviting ABANDONMENT in or any blocked emotion, acknowledging the emotion and asking it to leave and replacing the blockage with my Mother's LOVE is the Sacred Key for me in all my emotional clearings!

Margaret Arnett • Boulder, Colorado

In addition to opening up your connection to Spirit and relieving the stress on your body caused by trapped emotions, clearing unexpressed emotions is necessary for Ascension. In its simplest understanding, enlightenment means becoming lighter. That means the heavy, dense energies of blocked emotions have to go. You can't become lighter if you're holding heavy stuff.

Remember, anything fully expressed turns to bliss. Bliss is your natural state. When you're in bliss you naturally allow flow and connection with grace. Anything not fully released attracts more experience in order to get released and complete the experience. Holding dense layers of trapped emotions placed over other dense layers of trapped emotions is why so many of us on Earth feel separate from the Divine.

Another effect of keeping emotions trapped is our tendency to rationalize the maladies caused by the blockages. Nearly everyone thinks it's normal to grow old and die—when in fact stories of the ascended masters who have lived on Earth report their youthful appearances, even though they may be hundreds of years old. Those stories tell of masters who "die" consciously. They choose when to leave their physical bodies as they turn into beings of light and merge with higher densities of Source. The Western Bible tells us this is how Christ left the planet. Of course, his life and conscious death was so momentous that Christianity is one of the most practiced religions on Earth.

The Bible also tells of how both Elijah and Ezekiel left their earthly bodies in this manner. And if you read Eastern sacred books and the Vedas, you'll see many other stories of this kind of Ascension being reported by saints and sages. Because the energies of 3D have been so dense, few people can hold the thought of their soul being immortal and leaving our earthly bodies without dying. So we tell the story that growing old and dying is natural.

And it's not just the big stuff about which we make up stories in order to rationalize and then cut ourselves off from our spiritual essence. Thousands of published medical studies spanning nearly two hundred years show that 30 to 70 percent of the time any occurrence of an illness can be cured using a placebo—a sugar pill with no known medical value. But instead of our schools and media system telling us how powerfully able our consciousness is to cure disease, we're bombarded with a constant diet of how sick we are and how we need to take drugs in order to survive.

Consider how often you're witnessed, or participated in, a group of older adults getting together and then spending their whole time talking only about what illness they're dealing with and what treatment/drugs have been prescribed by the medical "professionals" who don't even acknowledge spirituality and conveniently don't bother telling you that you have a 30 to 70 percent chance of curing your illness simply by believing you're being treated for it.

Beyond the physical stories we tell ourselves to cope with the results of chronically unexpressed emotions, our entire mental health system rarely gives anyone the tools to relieve the psychological stress caused by suppressed emotions. You'd laugh if you heard this as often as I do. Nearly every time I guide someone through a process to clear trapped emotions that are causing them stress in the moment, the person I'm working with will tell me they've "dealt" with that before. Which of course begs the question, why is it still bothering you now?

Talk therapy and most popular methods of addressing emotional pain do little more than rearrange the deck chairs on the *Titanic*. Things are a lot neater, but the ship is still sinking.

And even loving platitudes like forgiving someone by understanding they did the best they could don't really solve the problem. It gives you a mental rationalization to attempt to mitigate your pain, but it doesn't remove the hurt. In fact, unless you complete the emotional component by fully expressing what arose during the experience, there will be no fertile ground for you to apply understandings like "they did the best they could."

On an even deeper level of understanding, forgiveness automatically takes place when the emotions caused by someone's actions are fully experienced. When you fully express the pain that was caused (whether by you or to you), then that energy is released. It's no longer in the field of the giving or receiving person. In essence, there's nothing left to forgive. I've taught numerous two-day courses in which, at the end of the first day, I led the participants through a process to heal their relationships with their parents. In every single one, I've had one or two people tell me that they haven't spoken with a parent for years, and that night after the process, their estranged parent would call them up out of the blue.

I once led a class through a process to heal relationships with their children. As soon as the process was finished, one woman announced that her daughter who had not spoken to her in four years sent her a text while she was processing! Forgiveness happens the instant the feelings from the experience are fully felt. Of course, owning your behavior and saying I'm sorry when appropriate always helps your relationships. But the object of what there is to forgive will have already been cleared the moment emotional energy generated by the experience is fully expressed.

Although it may not appear this way, the consciousness of Earth (Gaia) has already ascended to 5D. She's just waiting for us to catch up. She's part of the Spirit group that have temporarily dialed down Ascension energies so we're not blasted into blithering chaos all at once. Gaia is allowing the bridging energies of 4D to come to the planet in a measured way to make the transition as painless as possible for her beloved human children (that's us) given the circumstances of how much dense 3D energy is trapped in us. This is why so many people are getting the notion that there's more going on than they've been taught. It's very likely a reason you're reading this book. The energies of Ascension are nudging humanity forward. Hopefully this loving push will provide the impetus for millions upon millions of us to clear the dense trapped energies held in place by unexpressed emotions.

I've written this book to give you tools to take advantage of the newer energies and make your transition as easy as possible, given how much blocked emotional energy you may be unconsciously holding. And quite frankly, as 5D energies increase in strength on Earth, it's going to become more and more uncomfortable to hold the 3D energies blocked emotions are comprised of. Those who are stubborn will pass from illness and old age, only to continue their cycle of reincarnation on a different "earth" that is not in 5D. Those of us who embrace this change, especially while the energies of the planet are more accommodating, will have a much easier transition. Here's hoping you're one of those who choose to practice allowance for the Ascension miracle that is manifesting.

Getting to the Root Cause of a Trapped Emotion

Many people hold the understanding that karma is a punishment for past sins. They explain it as a way of being on the receiving end of things you've previously dished out so you can be balanced by experiencing the effects of what you've caused. There's a modicum of truth to this, but the reality is we live in a universe governed by laws of benevolence, not retribution. It is true that you reap what you sow. But there's no punishment involved in that equation. Just cause and effect.

As explained above, there's a self-regulating system built into the completion process of experience that requires your emotional response. Most of what we call karma is simply how this process plays out. If you don't learn the wisdom of an experience by completely expressing the emotions it evokes, an energy becomes trapped inside you that draws similar experiences in order to facilitate releasing the blocked emotions. This process is mostly behind what is commonly called karma. It's not retribution or balancing. It's simply receiving more of what has been denied so the experience can be completed.

Karma can be created in several ways: from incomplete experiences in past lives, from incomplete experiences imprinted from the time of our conception to birth, and from incomplete experiences during this lifetime. Karma can even originate from times after your soul emerged from Source and had not yet physically incarnated on a planet. The good news is that if you completely finish the emotion experience of the karma that was created in any of these times, it will automatically be cleared in the other places. So don't worry about how you access an emotion that arises during a clearing. Ninety percent of what takes place during a clearing is unconscious, so it doesn't really matter how you access a blocked emotion you're clearing. Spirit will do the heavy lifting once you open the door using the method described later in this chapter.

Another misconception about clearing work is that someone can do it for you. How many times have you heard someone say they saw a psychic and had this or that cleared from their field because of whatever the psychic did? My experience is that such "clearings," though well intentioned, don't really produce meaningful results. Sure, you may get some temporary relief, but without gaining the wisdom of having fully experienced the incomplete emotions, whatever symptom you've "cleared" will simply come back again.

You see, most of what a person says or does is the result of programming. Yup, operating programs that are running unconsciously. And for the most part, these programs are set in place by the time we're six years old—before most of our verbal and mental processing skills are developed. From the time of our conception until a few hours after birth, our consciousness isn't even fully connected to our bodies. During this period you pretty much pick up everything going on with your mom and her emotional field. That's when a lot of the unconscious programming that makes us who we are gets set into place.

And from birth to about age six, our minds are like a sieve. Most of the thoughts and energies around us pass right through, leaving more unconscious imprints on the character of who we express ourselves as in the world. Our relationships with our moms and dads (or whoever raised us when we were little) leave the biggest unconscious programs running our lives.

From birth to age six we have our operating systems pretty much installed for us. And as we form the mental abilities that give us the words to explain things, we make the assumption that "This is how I am." "It's my character." "I was born with these proclivities." When in truth, much of how we act in the world is just things we unconsciously learned from our parents who were acting out their own unconscious programs.

Because the imprinting process is unconscious, our minds will add explanations on top of the unconscious programming to make it easier to live with as we grow older. Some of these explanations can be helpful. But some are painful and get buried even deeper in our unconscious mind. For example, many of the people who do clearing sessions with me can sense they have self-esteem issues. And when we ask their unconscious to show them any beliefs associated with it, nearly all express something like "I'm not loved" or "I'm not lovable."

This can be further compounded into "I'm not worthy of being loved." "I'm not good enough." "I don't deserve love." Or in my case, when I first unpacked it, "God makes shit and I'm it."

To clear the programming, the feeling of not being loved has to be fully felt all the way back to the root of when it was first experienced. Because anything fully experienced turns to bliss, when the root experience of being unloved is fully felt, that energy is released and bliss can be felt instead. If you follow the steps outlined below, the unconscious programming that had been there running the show will be replaced by your Divine with auspicious qualities. That lack of self-esteem will be transformed into a deep inner knowing that you're connected to Source. And if you allow it, you can feel flooded with Divine love at all times.

I mentioned that lots of people I work with often tell me when we start a process that whatever we uncover is something they have already dealt with. A big reason the blocked emotional energy is still there, even though they supposedly dealt with it, is twofold. First, they were only made aware of what emotion was trapped, they never fully experienced it so it could be released. Second, they didn't allow Source to replace the unconscious programming (core beliefs) that our minds overlaid on those emotions. Remember that freight train analogy we used in describing our local minds at the end of the last chapter? This is another example of how our beliefs can keep running down the tracks laid by our local minds unless we actively invite our Higher Mind/Spirit to replace the unconscious programming directing it.

It's super important to replace any emotion you release with auspicious qualities. The good news is that it's very easy to do. You simply have the intent to connect with your Source and ask your Divine to do it for you. Don't go the route of letting your local mind control things. Your Spirit knows what you need and how to access it in the tangle of your unconscious. Just remember to complete each clearing by asking Source to fill the space that you've opened with auspicious qualities. It will know what you need better than your local mind can conceive. And when you open the door for it by clearing out the blocked energy occupying that space, your Spirit will quickly fill you with the auspicious qualities that will best serve you. All you have to do is ask for it and allow it to happen.

Also be aware that you're going receive more than you asked for. This is why it's important to let go of your concepts of right and wrong, what you have to do for gifts to come to you, and what's in the best, highest interest of everyone else. Your clinging to your unconscious mental programs will limit what you can receive, as Spirit will never violate your free will. If your moral code dictates this or that, those codes will limit what auspicious qualities Spirit can give to you. For example, if you believe that there's only so much wealth in the world, your unconscious programming may prevent your Spirit from giving you unlimited abundance because you may believe that if you get a heaping portion, then someone else will have to do without. But if you're willing to accept and allow that the universe, because it is benevolent, is an unlimited provider of abundance, then you'll have your coffers filled to the brim along with anyone else who allows theirs to also fill up.

This is why it's important to ask only for auspicious qualities when you allow Source to fill up the space you create by clearing a blocked emotion. And this is why it's also important to notice when your mind tells you that the blessings coming your way aren't possible or aren't real. For emotional clearings to fully transform you, you need to remember that you are a consciousness, not a mind. And then be aware as your local mind balks about what is possible for you to receive. Keep gently thanking your mind and reminding it that those beliefs may have been true when 3D energies ran the planet, but as we're Ascending, we're entering the age of miracles and wonders. Welcome them.

Here's an example of how a clearing process changed someone's view of their entire life:

> *Thank you for the clearing session I had with you. It was great to do a life review BEFORE I make my transition into what we call death. It was an honor to go*

back and look at my life from childhood into adulthood and clearly see how my emotions have attracted to me the same experiences in different forms and people and how you helped me to clear those emotions and move beyond them so that I can be free of the old baggage and emotional setbacks. After our session, I felt like a hundred pounds was lifted off of me and I felt light, free, empowered and definitely more conscious of my thoughts and emotions on a daily basis. I not only moved forward emotionally but also spiritually and what used to be a life remembered as confused, alone, powerless and resentful turned into a remembrance of love, beauty, appreciation and joy because I understood the different aspects of each experience and I saw the beauty and growth that comes with each experience after the clearing process. It was like a cleansing of the old way of thinking so the positive aspects and beauty of my life can come to the forefront of my mind. I am very blessed and fortunate for the clearing session with you and I thank you for playing such an important role in my ascension into higher consciousness.

Julie Sanchoo • Bronx, New York

The beauty of clearing a trapped emotion is that you're now free to write a new chapter for your life. Trapped emotions have a powerful energetic attraction that pulls similar experiences to you for as long as is necessary until you're finally able to fully feel the emotion being held and learn the wisdom associated with it. For many people it's as if they simply have the same kind of thing happening to them again and again. And because of your karma, you may spend lifetime after lifetime addressing the same kind of experience. Can you imagine your life (or all your lives) being a fantastic novel you're writing? But as soon as you finish the first chapter, you rewrite it over again. And again. And again. Clearing your blocked emotional charges allows you the freedom to finally write that second chapter. It allows for a whole new set of experiences to be had and wisdom to be gained.

Let's learn how to do it.

How to Clear Emotional Charges

This section will outline the basics of clearing blocked emotions. I'll offer instructions for deeper, more comprehensive processes in the third of the *My Ascension Handbook* series. But for now, we're going to learn the foundational steps of how this type of clearing is done. As you'll see when you read about Darryl's story at the end of this section, everything you'll need to radically transform will be described here. But if you should desire more help, later in this chapter I'll be listing a free, online guided process you can use. I will also be offering weekend intensive classes via Zoom every few months where you'll be able to release a big chunk of what you've been unconsciously holding your whole life.

The first, most important thing to know is not to clear your charges alone. Always invite your Divine to be there with you. Let go of the macho Western mindset that you can handle all your problems on your own, or that you're weak or somehow less than if you ask for help. The truth is your Divine is always with you. But the connection is amplified when you make it consciously with intent. Doing so allows you to receive more of the help that is always offered.

Acknowledge that your Divine is with you and then ask for its presence to connect. Your Divine lights up with joy whenever you do this, so don't only wait until you're in trouble to ask for help. Make it a regular practice and always do so before a clearing.

After you've invoked your Divine to be with you, here are four simple steps you can follow.

SEE IT

EXPERIENCE IT

ACCEPT & STAY WITH IT

REPLACE IT

That's it. These four simple steps are all it takes to transform your life. Practice seeing your emotions as they are, accepting them without judgment, staying with your emotions no matter how your mind tries to distract you as you fully experience the emotion. Then ask Source to replace what was there with something better. Practicing these steps will clear your blocked emotions. You'll reap the benefits of freeing yourself from destructive behaviors and repetitive negative mental programs.

SEE IT

Some trapped emotions are easy to identify. They'll show up automatically as "charges" that cause reactions in you. Other blocked emotions are buried deeper and you'll need to ask your unconscious to show them to you during periods of contemplation.

A charge is a reactive energy that gets frozen in place when you don't complete an emotional experience. As we've discussed, the nature of emotional energy is such that it seeks expression. Frozen emotional energy draws opportunities to you to allow its full expression. If you're quick to anger, or find yourself automatically responding in a certain way whenever someone does a certain thing, like cut you off in traffic, then you have a charge. If you've ever had someone say something in a certain way that really ticks you off, you clearly have a charge that is seeking expression.

Before my charges around secondhand smoke were cleared, I used to explode and let out hardy expletives to smokers who brought the smoke clouds of their addiction into my airspace.

Rather than respond to these situations, I would react, and words of anger would just come flying out of me. Having such uncontrolled reactions was a pretty good sign that I was holding a charge.

As I sat and contemplated the secondhand smoke experiences I was triggered by, I could see all the times in my early professional career when I was in a room so filled with smoke that I got ill. I remembered how I felt then, that I couldn't speak up to tell those people to stop smoking for fear of losing my job. So I toughed it out, feeling terrible for days and suppressing my feelings of helplessness deeper and deeper. The suppression of the emotions of anger, fear and helplessness early in my work career took hold as a deep-seated charge controlling my reactions twenty-five years later.

Now, you might react to this example with the thought, "Well secondhand smoke causes cancer so you had a right to react that way." Of course I had the right to feel that way. We all have the right to our feelings. But the difference here is that I was reacting, rather than responding. Other people might simply have asked everyone to please stop smoking. Or just left the room. Or changed jobs. All without the anger and swearing and compounded feelings of helplessness.

My wife found a woman very annoying in a spiritual community we were part of. There was a time for "personal sharing" during the service that was supposed to be something personal from your heart to uplift others. Every time this woman shared it was about trivial external things like, "Have you noticed my new boots?" "Do you like my new haircut?" Or some other story that's only purpose was to highlight how attractive people found her.

My wife finally realized she had deep charges with this woman and did a process to clear them. During the process she discovered that her anger came up because she did not allow herself any personal vanity, or to do things to draw attention to herself. Liberating herself from this self-imposed rule about vanity was a great gift. She did not become shallow, or spend too much money on clothes or makeup as she feared, but opened up lots of joy in allowing herself to express more of herself through her appearance. Often when we find someone annoys us, it's because they have or do something we do not allow ourselves to have or do.

Once a charge is formed, the attractive nature of blocked emotional energy causes people, places and things to align at every opportunity to release the stuck energy. Internally, we mentally compensate for the charge by saying it's just our "personality" or "that's the way I am." Externally we blame the other person for being so "inconsiderate" or point out how their actions are noticed by and disapproved of by others. But in reality, it was the charge that caused us to react the same way to certain situations over and over again.

I recommend you make a list of all your charges as you begin a systematic clearing process. They are the easiest to identify, so begin by writing them down. After you've listed your charges, take some time to contemplate. Set a timer for ten to fifteen minutes or play relaxing music without lyrics to keep time. You don't want to be distracted by thinking about how long you should contemplate.

Keep your charge list and contemplations brief. You are not journaling. You are just listing cues to help you later when you actually fully experience the emotion you will be releasing. List only a phrase or two to identify what the event was where you had that emotion, and then only a word or two naming the emotion. For example, entries on your list might be:

"Thirteen years old. Mom yelled at me about my bike getting stolen. I felt rage."

"Every time I drive by a huge mansion with ostentatious wealth on display, I feel angry."

"When I hear people who talk and laugh really loud, I judge them. I feel embarrassed for them."

"When people brag about their new car, I think they are stupid to spend so much instead of getting a used car."

"Eleventh grade. When other students got chosen to go abroad and I didn't, I felt crushed. They weren't very outgoing, didn't get good grades, and hadn't done as much to raise money for the program as I did, so why them?"

"My brother always got better grades than me without even trying, and my parents gave him rewards. I hate my brain."

"Whenever I see girls hanging all over guys just because they are handsome, I get jealous."

"Whenever it's a holiday I feel sad."

If you're not aware of specific charges you're holding, here's a technique that might help you find them. Find comfortable a position and do some deep breathing. Then scan your body to see if you find any place that is tense or feels like it is holding something stuck. Place your hands over that place and ask, "What is being held here? What could be freer? What could be easier?" You might find yourself having a memory of something that happened to you. You might suddenly remember a conversation that left you stressed without knowing why. Trust that anything that comes up, even if it seems vague, is a charge for you to put on your list to be cleared.

It's very important that as you allow these bits of awareness to come to you, you trust what is revealed. Put it on your charge list. Don't diminish it in any way. Even if it's not clear how that memory relates to anything, do not demand an explanation. Don't over think it. Just accept it as an insight and put it on your list. Many people have trained themselves allow doubts generated by local mind to run their lives. This makes them even further cut off from Source and its expression of intuition through their unconscious mind. In your early stages of identifying and clearing charges, please let the little nudges of insight come to you as unhindered as possible. If it shows up in your unconsciousness. Trust that it's important.

Once you've listed out the charges you're aware of, it's time to dig a little deeper. Ask your Divine to be with you, and then ask both your Divine and your subconscious to show you any blocked emotions you're holding that can be released. Let me stress once again, don't overthink it. Just add whatever comes up to your list of charges. Don't let your mind distract you by asking, "Why?" Or by trying to offer explanations or book-learned theories about psychology or behavior. Keep it simple. Just add whatever comes up to your list and then ask to be shown whatever is next.

You can do this around a specific topic, such as finances or health or some traumatic event in your life. Or you can just do it generally for whatever comes up. If you do focus on a topic, make a list of every time you can remember ever having any significant feelings about it. Even if you've already felt them, or cried about it, or had previously addressed it in therapy. Just note what happened in a phrase or two, and then write down the feeling you associated with it. When you get to the step of actually experiencing the emotion, any residue that was not previously expressed may present itself for release. Again, don't overthink it. Just note the experience and the feeling on your list and continue to contemplate for the time you've allotted.

For those of you who are new to accessing or describing emotions, here is a feelings wheel to help.

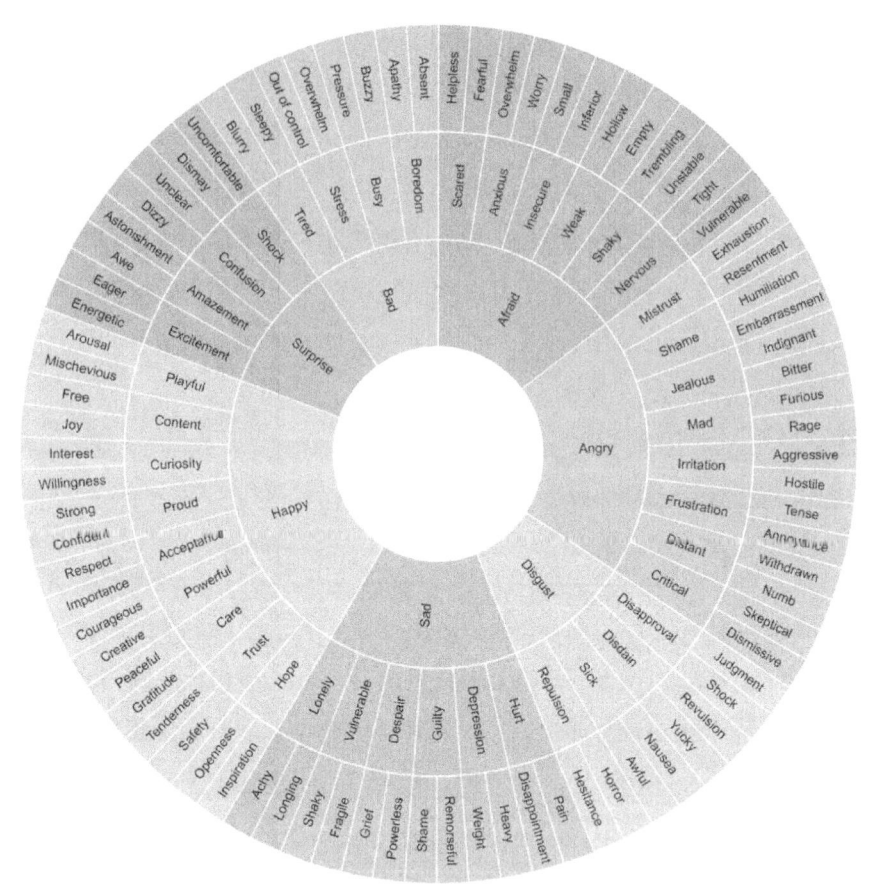

Start by doing your best to name the feeling that's coming up for you as you contemplate. Match what you discern to the feelings listed on the inner circle. Then breathe into the feeling and check the words in that area listed on the next ring out. Choose the word that best matches your feeling. Don't worry about what the words mean or whether the match is exact. Just trust your intuition to guide you. Then take another deep breath and check to see if any of the words on the outer ring of that section are a better match. If so, that's what you write down. If not, just stick with the word from the middle or center ring you have already identified.

Associated beliefs should also be welcomed as you contemplate. Ask your Divine and your unconscious to show you any beliefs that you may have associated with your blocked emotions and charges. Internal beliefs are most often associated with trapped emotions. These can be things like "I'm not good enough," "I don't deserve to have …," or "Something's wrong with me. I must be broken or damaged." External beliefs are most often associated with charges we're triggered by. Things like "So and so always does this," "Those people (or people in general) are this way, they just don't care about _____ like I do," or "They're bad or wrong because they _____."

To continue the example from above, after you've written: "Thirteen years old. Mom yelled about my bike getting stolen. I felt rage." You could add a corresponding belief like: "It's not fair. I always get blamed for things that aren't my fault."

"Every time I drive by a huge mansion with ostentatious wealth on display, I feel angry. Those people are using up too many resources for one family, while other people go hungry. Being wealthy hurts other people."

"When I hear people who talk and laugh really loud, I feel embarrassed for them. People shouldn't draw attention to themselves. Don't they know other people are making fun of them?"

Please remember that you're not trying to explain or understand your or anyone else's behavior. You're simply making a list of unexpressed feelings you're holding and the beliefs you've associated with them. Especially don't fall into the trap of trying to morally justify your belief system or condemn anyone else's. There's no right or wrong here. Assessing how people should or shouldn't act is just a mind game that will distract you from releasing your trapped emotion. The purpose of your contemplation is to see what's in you that's ready to release. It's not about justifying why you should feel that way. Keeping what you write as brief as possible is a good way to avoid the mind game of explaining why things happened and then applying a moral code toward it.

One useful thing to do during your contemplation is to locate in your body where the emotional blockage is being held. Emotions that are not fully expressed leave an energetic residue that is stored in various places in your body. Locating where they're held is useful for releasing the more difficult ones. If it's not obvious when your contemplation brings you awareness to a trapped emotion, here's how you can locate it.

Name the feeling. Then take a deep breath and say to yourself, "You are welcome here, _____." For example, if the feeling you've identified is rage, take a breath and say, "You are welcome here, rage." Then take a moment to be aware of your body. Notice if you feel a tightness, a tingle, or anything in your body. Again, don't overthink this. You will either feel something or not. And even if it's a very slight sensation that your barely notice, it means you felt something and located where you felt it. Jot this down on your list. For example, after you've written: "Thirteen years old. Mom yelled about my bike getting stolen. I felt rage. It's not fair. I always get blamed for things that aren't my fault," you could add: "Tightness in my throat," or wherever you noticed a sensation when you checked in with your body.

EXPERIENCE IT

First, try to eliminate distractions. Until you're comfortable moving your emotions freely, your mind will use any excuse to avoid feeling charges. It can be very helpful to find a place where you're alone, undisturbed, to release your charges. If there are others in the house and you're too embarrassed about releasing where they might hear you, lie to them (at least until you clear the charges you're holding about feeling embarrassed). Tell them you're practicing acting and will be working on emotional expressions. Then keep a pillow handy to scream into if it gets loud.

Also, have some tissues and a glass of water to keep nearby so you don't have any "reasons" to break out of your process if it gets uncomfortable. When you're set, dive in as best you can, knowing things will get easier and deeper as you practice more. Very few people do just one clearing for ten or twenty minutes and are completely done.

Once you've set up your space for clearing, invoke your Source to be with you. Don't try to process your trapped emotions alone. Imagine you're a small child holding the hand of your Divine. Keep Source with you throughout your process.

When you're set up in a safe place and your Divine is with you, it's time to begin your release. Experiencing a trapped emotion or charge means allowing it full expression. It means giving physical expression to the emotion. Laughing, moaning, wailing, sighing and growling are a few ways to give voice to emotions. Shaking, flailing, punching, kicking and crying are some of the ways emotions are given movement. There's no right or wrong expression of an emotion. It's also entirely possible to be completely quiet and still and be fully experiencing the feelings. For some people, all the sound or movement could be a distraction, or acting out how they "think" feeling anger should be, instead of just feeling it. Do what feels authentic and you will find your right expression. And because anything fully experienced turns to bliss, let it rip. Once you do, you'll experience the truth of this statement. And you'll know when you're on the right track because after you express a trapped emotion, you'll begin to feel more blissful.

When I first learned how to process emotions, I was told to commit to doing so for ten to twenty minutes a day. Ten minutes a day to thrive, twenty minutes a day to transform. If you're serious about changing your life, you'll commit to twenty minutes a day processing the charges and trapped emotions you've identified during your contemplations.

This process may feel yucky at first. In fact, a half-expressed emotion can feel worse than one that is totally suppressed. Stick with it. Soon you'll be completing your charges and experiencing more and more happiness in your life for seemingly no reason at all. As you release the attractive nature of the emotions you've been holding, you will open yourself up for Source energy to flow through you unhindered. That's where the causeless joy comes from—feeling alive and vibrant instead of continually reacting to the same old negative triggers unconsciously running your life.

Go ahead and set a timer or play emotionally moving music without lyrics for the period of time you choose for experiencing your blocked emotion. Pick the trapped emotion on the top of your list, or whatever is up for you that day. Invite your Divine to be with you. Then welcome the emotion. Actually say the words: "You are welcome here, _____." Just doing this may be enough to trigger the charge and begin your release.

If that's not enough, focus your breath and awareness on the area of your body that you located the charge being held in while you were contemplating it. Place your hands on that area and breathe into any knots, pains, or tensions in your body as you say the words welcoming the emotion. Often you'll experience a sharp stab of emotion when it first starts to release. Don't run from that. Keep breathing into the charge and see where it takes you.

If you're still not able to express the emotion, do some serious preparation before you try again. Squeeze your body as tight as you can, tensing every muscle group you're aware of. Hold the squeeze for twenty to thirty seconds and then relax. Repeat the squeeze and relax process three times in a row. Then breathe as quickly as you can in and out through your nose like you're doing the Ananda Mandala meditation. Breathe fifty or one hundred quick breaths if you can. Then put your awareness on your emotion. Welcome it to express. Place your hands on the area of your body you located it in, and breathe into it. Continue breathing and welcoming until you get some movement.

If nothing has yet happened after all this, fake it. You've seen a host of TV shows and movies where people got all emotional. Remember what they did and start doing that. Jump-start your process by making small sounds that you think a person expressing that emotion would make. Move your arms or your legs in little motions to start things up. As you continue to welcome the emotion and breathe into it, intentionally make some noises and movements. The release process will start, no matter how deeply buried the emotion is. You may have to give it two or three attempts before you get past faking it, but your body and mind will come on board after they see you showing them and encouraging them to do so—especially if you hold the intent that you welcome and allow the emotions to express.

And if need be, pray with your Divine for it to happen (remembering how prayer is done by seeing it has happened already and giving gratitude, rather than asking for it to happen).

Emotional expression comes in waves. And like a wave it builds up in intensity until it peaks and crests before dropping away. Allow these waves of emotion to form naturally once you begin experiencing releases. After a wave crashes, check to see if the emotion has been completely released. You can do this by breathing into the place in your body you located it and noticing if there's still any tension or tightness there. If it's completely gone, cross it off your list and immediately move on to replacing it with auspicious qualities. If it's not totally finished, take a moment to ask for and allow your Divine to fill up the space that has opened with light and love so that the remaining blockage can be more easily dissolved. Allow yourself to feel loved and appreciated by your Divine. Then either immediately give it another attempt to clear, or have a nice stretch and return the next day to complete it. The key when you're processing charges, is to stay with each one until it COMPLETELY burns out.

Please know that you may have suppressed memories and insights arise during your release. Don't shift your focus to the memories, they'll still be there after the charge clears. Stay with the emotion and keep breathing into and expressing whatever pain are being felt. If you wish, you can journal about your new memories that arose after you complete your process. Just don't interrupt the process by engaging your mind to write down insights that revealed themselves as you process. Stay with the emotional expression until it is complete.

While ten to twenty minutes of clearing is doable for many people, I want to acknowledge that for some people, their nervous and limbic systems are SO overloaded, that thirty seconds to two minutes might be where you need to start. If this is where you're starting out, imagine you are sitting on your Divine's lap and are being filled with endless, compassionate love for you, just as you are. Drink this in until you feel full and ready. Then ask your Divine to massage you with a golden oil that will calm your nervous system before you start. Ask your Divine to allow you to feel just enough of the emotion that you can focus on it without going into overwhelm. Then welcome the emotion into you and begin physically expressing it as described above. Stay with an emotion for whatever length of time you are able to hold it. Then celebrate with your Divine for the release you achieved, no matter how small. Celebrate with your Divine that you made an attempt at release, even if you did not experience one. And always ask your Divine to replace anything you have released with auspicious qualities as you celebrate.

If you only get a tiny chip of it experienced each time you attempt this, the walls holding your trapped emotions in place will eventually collapse. Please don't simply proclaim you can't do this, and then allow your mind to offer an explanation telling you it's not possible. With each pass you make, your total emotional "weight" goes down, allowing you to stay with the next experience a little longer. Be sure to do the "Replace It" step described below after every attempt you make to clear a trapped emotion, even if it feels like you had no movement or only a tiny bit of the suppressed emotion was released.

ACCEPT & STAY WITH IT

Until a person Awakens, his or her mind will rule the roost. The mind uses a variety of tricks to keep a person from fully experiencing a charge and completely releasing an emotion.

One technique to help you stay with the charges you're processing is to focus on the emotion you're feeling as getting bigger and bigger. A simple way to do this is on every breath, use intent and awareness to feel the charge as fully as possible. On every inhale say to yourself, "You are welcome here, _____." And on every exhale, say to yourself, "I allow myself to feel this even more deeply."

The joke my friends and I tell about this process is that if the pain ever gets so bad that it feels like a knife in your heart, grab the knife by the hilt and sink it in deeper! Look at your process like you're in surgery for cancer. You don't want to leave any bits behind for the disease to take root once again.

As you begin experiencing releases, be ready for tricks local mind may use to try to derail the experience so it can keep control. A common one is to spin your awareness into an obsessive thought loop. Guilt and shame are two common thought trains mind often use as an escape so you don't fully experience a charge. Don't buy into these. If you feel terrible about an experience you're remembering, that's great. Feel it. Feel the agony of such terrible actions as part of your clearing. But don't go into labeling yourself about what you did. It happened. That was the reality in the time and space it occurred. Given your state of consciousness, there's nothing else you could have done.

Rather than use these mental tricks to gloss over the experience, feel it completely so you can be done with it. Stay with the feeling, not with what your mind is telling you about what you SHOULD HAVE done or how you SHOULD feel about it. Mental awareness (or memory) of feeling is not the same as experiencing it. Because when your mind kicks in, your emotions will get trampled down.

Blame and judgment are the charge avoidance counterparts of guilt and shame. Rather than mentally turning inward to avoid feeling the charge, the mind turns outward with stories justifying why the charge hurts so much. "Look at what that person did to me," or "He's really an SOB for acting that way," our mind will say. Though these statements may be perfectly true, dwelling on them does not help move your charge. Rather they engage the mind, which in turn suppresses the emotion you're trying to clear.

Another trick the mind can play in order to avoid feeling a painful charge is giving you the idea that you should write down your experience while it's fresh. Journaling is a great tool for self-awareness, but as mentioned above, it's counterproductive when you're moving charges. It's just another distraction. Yes, you may have incredible insights as your charges clear, I certainly have. And memories, as far back as being in the womb, or from a past life, or even in between lives may start to show up. That's great! But don't write them down until you've completely finished experiencing the feelings suppressed by your charge. The mental activity of writing totally removes you from the emotional experience you're physically trying to complete.

If insights or memories do show up as you clear an emotion, acknowledge them then move on. Say to yourself, "Thank you, mind, for showing me this. I'll get back to you in an hour." Acknowledging the awareness will take some of the pressure off, dissipating its tendency for you to obsess over it. But immediately get back to feeling your feelings once you've acknowledged it.

Lastly, don't go into story. Powerful insights about why things have happened in your life will come to you as you process your charges. But don't dwell on them while you're in process. And don't let your mind step up when you first experience a charge by trying to explain to you why it happened. Insight from previous talk therapy, knowledge of your astrology, and platitudes of how your parents did the best they could when you were a child can all be explanations of how the charge first formed. As useful as this information may be, it won't help you clear your charges. Local mind tries to protect us from the emotional pain of charges by using awareness of this type of information as a buffer. Don't allow it. Acknowledge whatever thought or explanation comes to you, and then get right back to breathing into and feeling your charge.

Until you master the skill of flipping timelines (which requires you to be very clear of your suppressed emotions), there's really no other way to go through a blocked painful experience except to go through it. The bottom line is to simply be aware that: "This is what happened. There's nothing I can do about it." Don't feel bad about it, blame others for it, explain it, or write about it. Accept it. It's a reality and it's long past time you quit avoiding the experience of it.

The biggest reason people avoid processing charges is that they're just so darn scary. The emotions seem overwhelming, so we rationalize avoiding them. The solution is to understand that you're not alone facing them. Your Source is with you. Let it help you. If we could have cleared charges on our own, most of us would have done so long ago, because the benefits of being charge free are simply too awesome to ignore. But because the emotions behind stuck charges seem so debilitating, we need to enter the process holding the hand of something much bigger and more powerful—our God.

Consider how frightened a child can be when first encountering a new situation. But if Mom or Dad is there, holding the child's hand and encouraging them along the way, the child has a much easier time. That's what happens when you establish a connection with your Source and ask for help clearing your charges. Suddenly you're not alone. And no matter how big and scary the charge you're moving may be, Source is a whole lot bigger.

If you don't yet have a strong connection to Source energy (or if you want to strengthen the connection you already have), techniques for doing this will be presented in the next chapter. It's OK to start practicing those techniques as a way of enhancing your clearing. But don't give up on clearing. Don't wait until you have a clear conscious connection with your Divine before you move charges. The truth is your connection to Source can only get as strong as you are clear from the blockages that prevent you from receiving it. Your connection and your clearing go hand in hand. Practice them both if you want each one to grow, even if you only make a little progress in only one area at a time. That small opening will enough for you to eventually progress in the other area, which will in turn allow more progression in both of them over time.

Whenever I move charges, I invoke my Source to be with me and help me. And when the going gets rough, I turn it over. I acknowledge that I don't have what it takes to stay with this charge and I need help if I'm going to clear it. Source has never let me down. It's the intelligent energy from which physical reality is manifest. Of course it wants to help things run smoothly, so Source always helps whenever it's consciously invoked. And since blocked emotional energy creates resistance to receiving Source energy, Source is especially available to assist in clearing charges. There's no magic or special ritual to it. Simply invoke Source when you start moving your charges and allow the help to come to you.

And please remember, just because you are not yet feeling that Source is there helping you, does not mean it is not happening. The blockages and mental structures keeping your emotions at bay may be so strong that it may not appear to you that anything is happening. The reality is that Source energy is flowing through you or you'd be dead. And you not constantly feeling it is a sign of how far you've strayed from allowing your connection with Source to be felt, not that there is no connection there at all. Keep using Chakra Dhyana or Ananda Mandala meditation to raise your Kundalini. Begin practicing the steps in the next chapter about making your Divine your best friend. Then when you again attempt to move your charges, put your frustration with feeling cut off from Source and not being able to feel anything at the top of your list. Practicing moving charges again and again is the physical expression of you "allowing" the process to take place. Please stick with it, even if it seems like you don't get results the first few times you try.

As difficult as all this may seem, it is worth every single bit of effort. Be thankful that millions of people have come before you who have done some seriously heavy lifting. Gaia and her field are the lightest they've ever been, allowing clearing releases to be easier and quicker than ever before. I've worked with lots and lots of people who've told me immediately after learning clearing techniques all kinds of wonderful things happened. One person told me he suddenly got booked for very large interview shows and invited to numerous speaking engagements for a book he had previously released. He attributed this directly to techniques I taught in a class.

Check out what another beautiful soul told me:

> *I just want to say a huge thank you for an amazing clearing session yesterday. I was a little apprehensive beforehand as I honestly didn't know what to expect. After you left—I managed to complete ALL the emotions we identified. My body did some seriously weird contortions and spasms but, without letting go of my spirit mother's hand, I just filled right back up again in between each clearing and simply jumped into the next one. It was most definitely a roller coaster but was totally worth it. I was totally exhausted at the end but had the biggest smile on my face and felt lighter and freer than ever! I felt so empowered to be doing it myself, with support from my spirit family. I feel like something has shifted within me and I look forward to see what unfolds in the near future.*

Anji Wright • Thornton-Cleveleys, Lancashire, England

What did unfold after her shift was amazing! Anji told me she had previously dabbled in art on the side. And then suddenly friends noticed her work and got it placed in galleries. And just three months after the clearing session she described in the passage above, a gallery invited her to an art opening featuring her work. She's taking steps away from her previous job and becoming a full-time artist. Anji's now set to do what she loves to allow income rather than have a job to pay the bills so she could paint occasionally in her spare time.

REPLACE IT

This step is super important. Please don't bypass it.

After saying thank you, ask Source to fill you with auspicious qualities every time you clear a trapped emotion. You don't need to ask for specific personality traits or characteristics. After all, you just finished working so hard to clear out the old "personality" held in place by so many charges. You really don't want the new you to be limited by what you were able to conceptualize under your old mindset. Given the chance, your local mind will simply ask for your old characteristics to be returned so it can go back to being in control of who you are.

Trust that your Sacred Higher Self knows exactly what you need for your growth into awesomeness, as well as the timing and the order to give it to you.

Most of the clearing you'll experience will take place on an unconscious/etheric level. It's not like you're going to know what is really being removed and what it's being replaced with anyway. That's why invoking your Source and trusting in yourself is so important. Your Sacred Higher Self has been waiting for you to open this door by taking the effort to clear your blocked emotions. Remember, you have free will, so Spirit can't do anything for you without you asking. Practicing your ability to allow gives your Divine free rein to truly recreate a new you that you'll be happier with. Whole neural networks will be replaced. Memories will be uncovered and sometimes rewritten. You may even find yourself in a new timeline as a result.

No kidding!

Myself and many of my friends who make clearing charges a regular practice have all reported these things happening. For example, after clearing a deep pain caused by terrible actions another person did, it was no big deal for me to openly talk about what happened when I'd later run into the person who caused it. After all, the charge was now gone and I no longer harbored any animosity toward that person. But when I brought the subject up, these people would have no memory of it. They'd just look at me like I was crazy talking. After a while, I thought I was crazy, that all that psychology stuff about false memories was a real thing.

But then I started sharing what happened with my friends, and they too reported the same kinds of responses from people they had cleared charges about. Over time, and with the aid of my Sacred Higher Self, I came to realize we were now living in new timelines. We could remember the old ones, and if we chose to keep telling the story of what "happened" previously, we could recreate and go back to living in that old time. But in the new timeline, all the blocked energy holding that experience in place no longer existed. Hence the experience itself no longer existed in the new space I was occupying. And that's why the person who "caused" the experience in the old timeline had no memory of it in the new one. It had never happened in their current reality.

As you get more practice clearing charges, you'll understand just how limitless and powerful you really are. You'll begin to imagine futures of incredible potential and beauty. And you'll find yourself, from time to time, waking up in them. You'll naturally become more and more careful with your words. You'll stop telling stories about all the horrors of what happened, because you'll understand how they keep you rooted in those horrible timelines.

But for now, all you have to do is pause after every clearing and allow Source to fill you. Give it permission to do great works by asking it to fill you with auspicious qualities, replacing everything that was blocked with Divine love and light. Your part is to open the door by initiating the release through the vocal expression and physical movement of the stuck emotional energies that have held your old, undesirable experiences in a repeating loop. Source will seize the opening and do the rest once you give it permission to do so by asking.

You can enhance the process of asking by visualizing it. Imagine golden light coming directly from the Central Sun in a beam through the top of your head into your body. The energy is so powerful, you even feel your scalp tingle as the love and light enter you. As you inhale, sense this beam of golden Source light passing through your crown and going straight into your heart, lighting you up with its warm glow. And as you exhale, feel the Source light filter out from your heart through your entire body. See all the places where you had located the blockage you cleared now fill up with this auspicious energy. Continue this visualization until you feel full and comple

Spend five or ten minutes after every clearing to allow Source to do its thing. I prefer to ask Source to fill me with auspicious qualities and then just lie back and relax, knowing it's taking place. And besides, it feels so good to imagine myself bathing in a light bath of pure, Divine love.

I'm tired of always *reacting* to the events in my life based on childhood triggers. I'd rather *respond* to each unique situation I encounter using the full range of possibility available to me. It makes each experience new to me. It puts me into a place of wonder—living, rather than existing. That's why I ask for auspicious qualities from my Source. When I'm connected to everyone and everything by embracing Source energy, the qualities infusing my consciousness are so much greater than the limited codes and ethics my mind can invent or learn from others. And it feels a whole lot more pleasant and invigorating as well.

Practice these four simple steps if you want to let go of troubling patterns in your life and start living in freedom and bliss. Keep a charge list and spend time every day clearing. Ten minutes a day to thrive. Twenty minutes a day to transform.

As charges clear, be ready to experience a new freedom. Instead of held tension and conditioned reactions to life, happiness and a relaxed response to events in the world will become your normal state of being. Because charges are so loaded with scary emotional content, most of us have been raised to avoid moving them. What no one's ever taught you is that anything fully experienced turns into bliss. Once a charge is cleared, happiness takes over. And the more charges you clear, the greater your happiness will be. The effect is cumulative.

Since I often become aware of my charges during a business meeting, while in traffic, or at some other time when I may not be able to fully experience it, I keep a charge list. I make a mental note of the charge and set an appointment with myself to clear it later that day when I'm not in public. Or I jot down my charges whenever I'm aware of them. I'm aware that strong negative emotions I'm experiencing are probably rooted in charges, so I stay alert to that experience being a signal that another charge is ready to be moved. If the negative emotion is reoccurring, it's definitely a charge. So I put it on my list.

Don't be surprised if your charge list grows longer before it gets shorter. Clearing one set of charges often opens your awareness to several others that were buried beneath it. Accept that you have a whole lifetime of emotional blockage backlog and it may take a concerted effort for a period of time for them to all clear. But for most people, if you commit to daily clearing for a month or two, you won't even recognize yourself because of the wonderful changes you'll have allowed to take place. Of course this is a huge commitment. But weight out your options. A month or two of serious clearing work versus a lifetime of pain and suffering? Which will you choose?

Lastly, please remember the teachings about mind in the last chapter. You really need to make friends with and then set clear boundaries with your local mind if you want to receive the full benefit of this clearing work. First and foremost, remember you are consciousness, not your mind.

Stories of Transformation

Darryl's transformation was the first time I saw someone's body, in addition to their life circumstances, change for the better because they worked at clearing emotional blockages. I met Darryl when I taught a class in Alamogordo, New Mexico. Darryl was bent over and his movements were stiff and slow. He used a cane to walk. His personality was gruff, almost abrasive in the way he spoke. Over the weekend class I led several group processes, taught how to move charges and initiated Awakening for those in attendance. At the end of class I gave everyone my phone number and asked them to call if the going got rough and they needed more help. It was just a normal Oneness Awakening class for me.

A little under two weeks after the class, Darryl called. He was very upset and asked me what he needed to do to feel better. All his charges were up as he was only able to partially release the charges on his list when he tried processing them. He told me he was spending at least twenty minutes a day processing his blocked emotions and wanted to know if he was doing it wrong or what else he could be doing. He said he was feeling worse, not better. I told him to keep moving his charges. That was it. That was all he needed to do. If he hung in there, it would clear up and he'd feel much, much better.

He was angered by my response. I told him to stick with it anyway.

I didn't hear back from him after that.

Six months later I traveled back to Alamogordo again to lead a deeper clearing process for people who had taken the first class. As I was preparing to start the process, a man I didn't recognize walked in. He introduced himself as Darryl. I was stunned!

He was standing upright. He moved with ease and grace. He still had a cane, but used it more like an actor holding a stage prop than a person leaning on it to walk. I asked Darryl what happened. He told me he just kept moving his charges as I had encouraged him to do.

After I finished the process I was leading, I spoke with several people who knew Darryl. They all said they couldn't believe how he'd changed. They said they used to not be able to stand being around him, but now he's a pleasure to be with. His language and speech changed. He was no longer gruff and angry. They now actually looked forward to the times they were with him, instead of avoiding the get-togethers they knew he'd be attending.

This was the transformation I observed Darryl undergo as he chose to rigorously process his emotional blockages. There's no limit to who or what you can become. Your "reality" only seems fixed in place because the attractive nature of trapped emotional energies keeps it that way. Clear your blockages and anything is possible. You can literally have it all, because your true nature is consciousness. Consciousness resides in the field of All That Is, because consciousness is made from and exists as All That Is. Free yourself from the limits imposed by held charges and you'll experience your expansiveness. It's who you are. Truly, who you are.

Here's another story of transformation. I really liked that Tibor was able to come so far, so fast, even though he previously had almost no experience identifying, let alone feeling his emotions.

Let me start from the time that I discovered Peter. I was at a period in my life where I felt like I was doing the same routine day in and day out. Trying to chase the money, thinking that if I was able to provide more for my family then that would bring happiness and fulfillment. My wife and I have four kids altogether. She had two girls from a previous marriage and together we had two children. A girl and a boy. We have been married for ten years now. By this time, we had become accustomed to negative conditioning and behaviors that caused a lot of resentment and ill feelings. We were not getting along and it wasn't getting any better. We are both dealing with addictions and trying to hold the family together. When I discovered Peter on YouTube I was intrigued by his story and the fact that he wrote addiction literature. It gave me hope that he could help. The other fact that told me he was sincere is that he offered sessions on donations only basis. In my opinion, that told me that he really was here to help! I was literally on the brink of divorce. I really wanted to turn things around but I didn't really want to go the traditional therapy route because it hasn't worked in the past. I eventually convinced my wife that we should do a coaching session with Peter. She agreed and we booked a session. The only problem was that the session was about four weeks away. We booked it and at the same time I noticed that a new class was about to begin in a week. I was worried that if my wife and I didn't started working on the relationship now, we might not make it to the coaching session. I wrote Peter an email asking if he could take us on for the weekly class meeting over the next six weeks? He got back to me so fast and agreed to let us join on a donation basis. Even though the class was more about abundance blocks I felt like this was something my wife and I could do together and even if there was one small subtle piece that I gained from Peter that would help my marriage, I took it! When I did a life coaching session with Peter I realized that I had been holding on to a lot of emotions and negative conditioning from childhood. As we were doing the session I was struggling to describe my own emotions and inner feelings. I have never really talked about them with anyone so I found it a little difficult to vocalize my own feelings. I needed someone to guide me and give me an example of how to process and release these trapped emotions. So the class that we took with Peter as well as the coaching session made me realize that I didn't know how to describe what I'm feeling on the inside. I was like a child throwing a tantrum because I was upset with someone else's behaviors and could not express it in a healthy manner. I can say that my coaching session with Peter showed me how I've been suppressing my emotions and now I can see how they have impacted my *relationships as well as my decisions. That has led me on my own discovery of self-realization and being able to vocalize my feelings to my spouse. This aspect of emotions has completely saved my marriage! It has not been easy, but worth it. After doing a lot of research on my own about emotions and being able to communicate them I noticed that I was getting triggered by things that didn't bother me before. I think this is a natural part of expanding your awareness. Now I'm recognizing how my emotions have clamped down on my consciousness and were controlling my life. The more I learn, the more I realize how much deeper the rabbit hole goes. I'd like to be clear that nobody is going to do the work for you. You heal yourself, Peter is just guiding you. The good thing is that Peter has multiple tools that you can choose from if one doesn't resonate with you. I think that this has been a gradual process that can only begin once you choose to have a life free of suffering. I thank you so much for really opening my awareness so that I can heal myself!*

Tibor Szalka • Cartersville, Georgia

If you're wondering if this process will work for you, even if you're a skeptic who doesn't believe in all the woo-woo stuff in this book, please check out Milton's story. I met Milton through a house-sitting service. We interacted only briefly before he spent two weeks looking after our cats while my wife and I vacationed on the beach in Mexico.

I met Peter when I was at a particularly low point in my life—professionally, financially, socially, pretty much every aspect. I didn't mention that to him, and he didn't push his clearing or spirit guiding on me at all. A few weeks later I don't know why, but I was motivated to watch some of his videos. I've always been intrigued by the spiritual realm, and somewhat open to whatever applications and practitioners I encounter in it, but I'm also a pretty skeptical person and so didn't really have much expectation. A few more weeks went by and then I reached out to him and asked about a session. We ended up doing two clearings, over a few weeks. Again, I was skeptical, and while I didn't feel anything immediately or tangibly transformative in the moment, they did bring up some important and impactful things that I had been carrying with me for many, many years. I did feel that some things were indeed "cleared," or more accurately, at least for me, I was able to think back about certain significant events and people in my life with a greater clarity and much happier perspective. Nothing immediately changed, though, I just continued on with my life as I had been doing for, well, the past many years. Then over the next several months everything changed! I met someone for the first time in a LONG while, with whom I connected on a deeper level than perhaps I ever have before. I have said to her more than once that if my friends could have created the perfect person for me—with all my quirks and diverse interests—she would be it. In addition, my professional and financial lives improved radically. I wasn't doing anything different, at least not that I could tell, but things just started working for me—things I had been doing for a long time that always seemed to have promise but came to naught all of a sudden began paying off. I was in a position where I literally couldn't afford to fully fill my gas tank and had to be highly selective in what I could buy in a grocery store, and now I could pay for peoples' dinners and buy gifts for my friends who had been so supportive of me through my dark times. Not long ago Peter and I did a Channeled Spiritual Coaching Session and that was also transformative. I not only brought forward and thought about all the trauma in my many decades of life, but I was told to fully embrace them. So I did, and in so doing I reconnected with my long-gone parents, and I realized that so many of the negative emotions and perceptions I was accepting as my reality all had exact opposites and those were the reality I was truly living—I didn't have limitations, I had unlimited potential; I wasn't rejected, I had many friends in my life who were supporting me, respecting me, appreciating me, and so on. And now I can frequently draw on what I learned and experienced in each of our sessions, and use that to clear my perspectives and embrace every day!

Milton Lewin • living a nomadic life!

I particularly loved how nothing outwardly changed in Milton's life, but because the trapped emotional energies were released, he was no longer blocked from receiving the bounty his Divine had been trying to send to him all along.

Before listing some of the resources I've prepared to help you clear your blockages, let me go into more detail about a couple of the finer points of clearing charges. People ask me all the time if they can clear everything all at once. Many wonder why I insist they give each and every blocked emotion its due. You see, even though there's really only a handful of emotions at the core of a person's blockages, the attractive nature of trapped emotional energy generally causes a multitude of experiences to build layer upon layer of incompletions during a person's lifetime.

During contemplation it's vital to get to the "root" cause of where the emotion was first placed in your unconscious. As we discussed earlier, that usually took place before six years old or in a past life. But in addition to clearing the root, every time you trigger that trapped emotion during a subsequent experience in your life, you create another layer of dense energy that's held in your body. My experience is that a single mass clearing of all the times you've held a trapped emotion never completely removes the whole pattern from your unconscious. Sure, you'll get some relief, and may even be able to clear the root cause, but the other pockets of dense energy held in your body will simply keep attracting negative experiences to you in an effort for them to be cleared as well.

If you don't systematically address them, you can find yourself unconsciously reliving the very patterns you thought you had cleared.

That's why I believe it's important to be thorough and give every trapped emotional experience you can identify its due. Remember the cancer removal surgery analogy. The surgeon doesn't want to leave any bits behind that can grow back.

Another part of the puzzle is that trying to clear your charges in bulk bypasses an important part of the process. You see, trapped emotions that have been unexpressed for so long usually need some coaxing to release. By suppressing a feeling (whether intentional or not), the message has been sent that the feeling is not welcomed. Whether it's because you're afraid of it, or simply because you judged that you don't like how it feels while it's expressing, the emotion has learned not to show up or else you'll heap even more disapproval and abandonment on it. And you thought it was just you that was dealing with a root cause of not being loved or lovable?

Uh-uh.

Your emotional body and your unconscious mind know the abandonment and feeling of not deserving love all too well. They are etherically mirroring exactly what you are physically suppressing. This is why you may need to go slow and spend time coaxing out trapped emotions when you first begin. Your emotional body and unconscious are just as afraid of expressing what is blocked as you have been of allowing them to express it. So be patient, and treat your emotions (or inability to access them) with the same loving care you'd give a sick child who needs to be nursed back to health. Shower yourself with love and approval for every attempt you make and every little bit of progress you achieve.

And when the dam finally breaks, let it. "You should have let your head explode!" as one monk advised a classmate of mine after a particularly big clearing process. You'll still be totally there when the expression is complete.

Have you ever seen a small child scrape their knee? Unless their parents shut them down, they'll cry like it's the end of the world! But after a few minutes, the charge is completely gone. They're totally laughing and playing because the hurt is over and done with. You too will feel this way when you're able to allow complete expressions of previously trapped emotions. Just remember to love your charges. It's their nature to be scary and painful. Appreciate that about them and let them express as they want to express.

Lastly, I've yet to experience having charges successfully cleared when another person said they were doing it for me. I've seen a lot of psychics and spiritual healers in my day. Many told me of all kinds of darkness they could identify in my energy field. No kidding, I thought. My life sure felt like a struggle until I was led to the clearing techniques I've shared here. Many of these healers did what they know how to do after I paid their consultation fee. I have nothing but appreciation for each and every one of them. But truth be told, their clearings didn't work.

Or maybe they did, and they just didn't stick.

Now that I can speak about clearing with my Sacred Higher Self, I know why. You see, even when denser energy was successfully removed from my field, I never gained the wisdom of what the energy had to teach when it first entered my field. You see, without wisdom setting in, an experience is not complete. And I don't mean some kind of wise saying, adage or "life lesson" I can mentally provide after completing an experience. By wisdom, I mean the energetic pattern of completion is in place. That experience is complete. I don't need to have it again unless I enjoyed it and desire to relive that joy.

This kind of completion energy can, if you wish, be turned into a mental experience. But I've learned that the more I process my experiences through my mind, the more removed those experiences become from my life and the less joy I feel about them. Either way, I can always choose to remember an experience. But the memories are always less than the experience itself. And the more I fixate on explaining past experiences, the less space I have for new experiences—which are less blissful. The very act of remembering takes me out of my true nature of being a consciousness and causes my focus to be in the diminished state of experiencing through my mind.

I know this is a bit complicated to try to explain, so I'll leave it at this. If I'm not the One who learns wisdom from completing an experience, then the experience is not truly complete. Another person can't do it for me. They can guide, direct and encourage. They can sit with me and hold space for me as I do it. But I'm the One who has to do it if I want to be the One who grows as a result.

While reviewing this book, Tracy, my wife, added some of her experiences to emphasize that getting support to help you clear an emotion is different than getting someone to do it for you.

Most of us were raised to believe that we should be able to do things for ourselves, that only weaklings ask for help. Tracy's process sped up greatly when she gave herself permission to have others create a container for her to do work within. Having loving, supportive people surrounding her as she went through her emotional charges allowed her to go deeply very quickly. And, it also ensured she wouldn't chicken out!

One tool Tracy used was to have a support group that met weekly. She was in counseling with her first husband during that time. She came across some deep rage when she encountered ways her husband mirrored all the disregard and disempowerment of women she experienced her whole life. The therapist told her husband to prepare himself for what would likely be a year of anger as she went through this. Later that week her support group held space for her as she let herself fully immerse in all and feel all the dynamics of masculine dominance. After each wave of emotion, they would encourage her to breathe and take in love for a few minutes. Then they asked her to explore, "Is there anything beneath anger?" She went through many layers of emotions that day but ended in peace. The next week her therapist was amazed that she was no longer triggered by masculine-feminine power struggles. What a traditional therapist said would take a year, Tracy completed in one session. Having support to help you do your work can be a powerful blessing!

This is an area where it's important to be authentic. If having someone help with holding space for you to release is better for you, make it happen. Maybe you have a friend who is wanting a lot of personal growth now and would like to take turns supporting each other. Just be sure to follow what's outlined in this book. If your friend is trying to analyze or explain your feelings, it will take you out of your process and sabotage your release. If you don't have a skilled friend (or one willing to buy this book and commit to this technique), it's probably better to sign up for a session at becomingawesome.one/session. Bottom line, there is nothing weak about getting support. It takes courage to let others witness you dive into darkness. After using the support group for a while, Tracy eventually found it was easier to clear when she did it one-on-one with just her and her Divine. Trust yourself. You'll find what's right for you.

Resources to Help

Here're some of the tools I've produced to help you clear your emotional blockages.

Start by visiting my Becoming Awesome website. It's at https://becomingawesome.one/

There you can book coaching and guided clearing sessions on a donation basis, so don't worry if your abundance isn't flowing as much as you wish at this time. A guided session can be helpful because you'll have guidance for identifying blocked emotions if you're unaccustomed to doing so. You'll also benefit from being assisted by the energy field of your guide, who has already cleared much of what they're holding. When you're at the becomingawsome.one website, click on the Sessions tab to book a process. It's at https://becomingawesome.one/session/

I've also produced a video of a guided sixteen-minute process to help you clear a charge once you've identified it. The video is freely provided and you won't have to wait for a session opening if you use it. You can view the video on Rumble.com. Search for "Clearing Charges Exercise to Release Fear, Anger & Negative Emotions." Or you can find it at this web address: https://rumble.com/v10rv1p-clearing-charges-exercise-to-fear-anger-and-negative-emotions.html

At least four times a year I'll be teaching a weekend class via Zoom about all the concepts and processes covered in this book, as well as other special practices for you to get even more Ascension skills than what this book covers. A big advantage of taking a class is you'll be immersed in the group's energies. It will make your clearing processes deeper and easier. Plus, I and others who have done extensive clearing work will be present, lending our consciousness around clearing to the energetic field created in the class to assist you. Many people find that the group environment of these classes really opened up layers of blockages they were not able to previously access.

And rather than drag things out, you'll make a whole lot of progress over a single weekend if you choose to take a class. It can really accelerate your growth arc. Please click on the Classes/Events tab on the Becomingawesome.one website to find the dates and register for a class. It's at https://becomingawesome.one/events/

I also have several recordings of individual processes I've led available for free on the Processes page of the Becomingawesome.one website. Click on the Processes tab for the list of what's available. These are at https://becomingawesome.one/processes/

Just this book alone will give you everything you need to clear your past and embrace the future you desire. All the resources available at Becomingawesome.one are there to offer help and support to accelerate your process.

And please don't think that what I've outlined here is the only way to transform. There are many powerful teachers and techniques available, with more being uncovered every day. Find what's right for you. If you resonate with what's written here, that's a pretty good sign that you're on the right path for you at this time.

Ascension is coming to Earth. We're well past the point where it can be stopped. How quickly and how profoundly you enjoy the benefits of Ascension is up to you. What are you willing to do to allow yours to manifest quickly, in a big, big way?

Ten minutes a day to thrive,

twenty minutes a day to transform.

Step 3 – Invite Your Sacred Higher Self Into Your Life

To celebrate that we're bringing the Divine into our lives, I'd like to share the translation of the invitation from the goddess Sekhmet, which is written in gold at the entrance of her temple in Karnak, Egypt.

> *I only ask you to enter my house with respect. To serve you I do not need your devotion, but your sincerity. Nor your beliefs, but your thirst for knowledge. Enter with your vices, your fears and your hatreds; from the greatest to the smallest, I can help you dissolve them. You can look at me and love me as a female, as a mother, as a daughter, as a sister, as a friend, but never look at me as an authority above yourself. If the devotion you have for any god is greater than the*

devotion you have for the God within you, you offend them both and you offend the ONE.

I love how Sekhmet welcomes us no matter where we are at. And even though she is a Goddess, she teaches that the God within you is the One God. Let's ponder a deeper understanding of the God within and where it resides.

Allow me to introduce you to the concept of *Antaryamin*. In Sanskrit, it means "inner witness." It's the indweller, or observer. Remember how earlier I described your being as consciousness, existence, bliss? Antaryamin is an ancient term recognizing you as that consciousness that blissfully exists. If you recall the explanation I presented of how we act as God's eyes and ears to expand creation, the Antaryamin is that part of you that is God that is observing through you. It's why completing an experience by fully expressing your emotional response is so important. It's requisite to you being a clear enough channel for God to witness your experience of cocreating the moments of your life.

Antaryamin can also refer to the Higher Self or the power of the fractal of God expressing as your soul. Because much of connecting with soul is done through unconscious faculties, I'd like to present a metaphor to help you better access your soul connection. Appreciating this analogy will help you open up the clear, conscious contact with Source you're seeking.

We build all sorts of magnificent temples across the world as places of worship. But if your Antaryamin dwells within you, shouldn't it have its own very nice temple to reside in you? Most everyone is familiar with the concept that our bodies are a temple, and we should treat it as such. Now let's carry it a step further and engage the creative power of our unconscious and actually build a temple in our bodies. Let's place it in our hearts, because lots of new research is showing the heart has its own network of neurons. And researchers tell us the electromagnetic field generated by your heart is five thousand times stronger than the one generated by your brain.

I encourage you to have a little fun. Take the time to build a temple in your heart. Design it in detail. Draw color pictures of it if you wish. Write a story describing what it looks like. Map out a floor plan with each and every room in your temple.

Take the time to decorate each room. Imagine the colors, how you'd furnish it, and any special features of each room. Let your imagination run wild!

One of my friends put an antigravity room in his temple with trampolines covering the floor, ceiling and walls. When I asked him why, he said because it would be fun!

Another friend had a teleportation pad in one room, because she wanted to be able to go anywhere, with her Divine traveling right along with her. It's your temple and your Divine. Put everything you desire in it. Even a treasure room if it makes you happy to know that you have access to unlimited wealth through your connection to Source.

And while you're at it, don't forget the outside of your temple. What does it look like? What is it made of? There's no right or wrong answer, there's only what inspires your imagination and makes your heart sing.

Where is it? Mine is on a small island with a beautifully manicured lawn above rocky cliffs rising above a turquoise blue sea. It's always sunny there. The air is crisp and clear allowing me to see the sparkly waves through the tall glass windows for miles and miles. Is yours on a mountaintop? In a sacred forest? Perhaps it's in a beautiful oasis hidden away in a sandy desert?

Have you ever experienced a guided meditation where you were asked to go to a beautiful place that you found calm and relaxing? Why not put your temple there? All of creation is available to you. Imagine your happy place and then use this exercise to permanently "fix" that energy into your heart.

During one of the months I studied at Oneness University in India, the monks had us work on building a temple in our hearts for a couple of hours a day during an entire week. At the time I didn't think much of it. Sure, it was fun to use my imagination to feel happy, but I honestly thought it was just something to do that would give us a break from all the hard work of clearing emotional blockages day after day. Little did I realize that the temple I built would be instrumental when I moved from being empathetic and occasionally sensing things to becoming a full-fledged channel who could speak with any consciousness I could identify.

A couple of years ago, I was taking an online course on how to remote view. I was slogging along, occasionally being able to correctly identify my target locations, but for the most part just spinning my wheels. Then I saw a video of a remote viewer saying how his skills sharpened tremendously when he had a Quantum Healing Hypnosis Technique session based on Dolores Cannon's work. I found a local practitioner and booked a session. Once the session started, everything took off. I stopped following the guidance being given by the therapist and went where my unconscious took me—into the temple I had built in my heart a decade earlier—a place I had completely forgotten about since then. While in my temple, I started conversing clear as day with a Pleiadean named Mira. She told me she was part of the "ground crew" of our star family from the Pleiades. Her job was to find people like myself who were ready to embrace 5D skills like channeling and to help them.

The therapist did her best to keep up with me describing my surroundings and the conversation I was having, as I had long since stopped following her direction for the session. When I was complete and came out of the light trance she guided me into, she asked me all kinds of questions about where the place was I went to. She was boggled trying to understand that it was in my heart. That it was a place I had already built in detail years before. I too was stunned, because until I started writing this book, I never really understood the power of having a dedicated "space" inside my heart for my Divine to live. Because the place was already prepared, it was easy for me to "go there" and open up to communication from other entities that can access nonphysical realms.

Consider having a comfortable lounge or conference room in your temple just so you'll have a place to greet and converse with all the entities you'll like to channel after you establish clear communication with your Higher Self

I'm deeply grateful that Mira presented herself to me and helped me refine my abilities once they opened up. I'll speak more about her help later in this chapter. For now, I just want to introduce you to the concept that there's a lot of help available from many, many benevolent entities once you open yourself to receiving it.

Before we get into the practical steps you can take to open up a clear line of communication with your Sacred Higher Self, here's one last note about building a temple for your Antaryamin. The temple you build for your Divine to dwell in doesn't have to be inside you.

Some people create an altar in their homes, knowing it's a place for their Divine. Doing so can be very powerful. *Sri Murthi* is a Hindi term for an icon of a God that has the consciousness of that God in it. I've seen very devout people who have Sri Murthis that emanate sacred substances. In India, some people report that honey, ghee or turmeric pour out of the photos they have of Divines, collecting in bowls placed at the base of their photos. Others use their Sri Murthis as a portal to speak directly with their Divines. I've felt some pretty powerful energy fields when I've been in front of these. And I have friends in the US who use their Sri Murthis to allow their Divine to "charge" bottles of water with what they call Soma. When I drank the Soma, I was immediately thrown into an enlightened state that lasted for hours. It also raised the baseline of my awareness such that I experienced the beginning energetics of enlightenment 24-7.

And if all this sounds strange because it's from India, consider the encyclopedias of "miracles" chronicled by Catholics, like the shrine in Lourdes that has healed many since a young girl had a vision there of women in white during the 1800s. Or the many "weeping" statues of the Virgin Mother reported to be in Catholic churches around the world. All this goes without even mentioning the Western traditions around "holy water" and the sacraments it is used for.

In addition to altars with powerful representations of their Divines, some people even treat their Divine like a living, breathing person who dwells in their home with them. Some have a room set aside with a bed in it for their Divine to sleep in. Some prepare meals for their Divine, setting an extra plate out when they eat and scooping portions onto it. Sounds crazy, huh? But should you ever meet a person who does this, ask them about their lives. Things we see as unimaginable miracles are everyday occurrences for them.

I don't go so far as having living quarters in my house for my Divine. I'm totally content feeling the connection in my heart—one that was amplified by my having built a temple there. I do, however, take extra time to keep my house as neat as I can, knowing that my Divine is always with me. And I want my house to be as inviting as possible for my most amazing guest.

Make Your Divine Your Best Friend

Just this concept alone stands on its head the traditional relationship most people have with God. First, it makes God personal to you. It's no longer about what the great teachers and holy people say about how to relate to God. It's how a friendship with your BFF looks for you. Think about having a friend who is so pleasurable to be around that connecting is the first thought you have whenever you're doing something you love. And then imagine what such a relationship can look like for you.

Here are a couple of examples of how people who have a great relationship with their Divines interact with them. While taking classes at Oneness University, I often spoke with a monk I related to. I called him Honey Bear because he was a huge man with the lowest, sweetest, most soothing voice I had ever heard. Every morning before class he'd lie prostrate at the altar set up in the classroom for a period of time before he'd start the lesson. We were discussing how to create a relationship where the Divine is your best friend. Since I would never even consider lying prone at the feet of my best friend to say hello in the morning, I asked him why he did this. He told me that his best friend has the power to create universes. He was just showing a little respect for a being of such magnitude. His recognizing this by lying prostrate in no way diminished his friendship.

Seeing him do this was an important learning for me. Rituals are neither good, bad, necessary or unnecessary. It's all about what you bring to their performance. Some people really like rituals, as they can become a physical shortcut to enter an expansive state of awareness that celebrates the connection taking place. My takeaway was that it's not the ritual that's causing the connection, it's what the person participating in it brings that matters.

Now contrast this type of expression of one's Divine being their best friend with that of a Catholic priest in India many considered to be a saint. One of my teachers went to visit him and found him in a run-down building he called his church. The monk met the priest and offered to take him out to lunch, having noticed the financial condition he appeared to be in. The priest told him that was not necessary, his friend would bring them lunch soon. The monk and the priest then had a wonderful connection. But after some time, the monk was getting hungry and again offered to take the priest to lunch. The priest told him not to worry, lunch was coming. He had asked his friend and it was taken care of.

A few more minutes passed and then a dog walked through the building. It had a paper bag in its mouth. The dog dropped the bag and then scampered off. In the bag were two hot dosas, loaded with steamed vegetables.

I love this story because the priest was in constant contact with his "friend." He knew the dosas were on their way because he simply checked in when the monk told him he was hungry. And the priest never wavered in his faith of knowing his connection was solid. He was so secure in his trust that his Divine using a dog to deliver (or acquire?) his lunch was just another normal thing in his day.

For me, the closest I ever felt to people was when I was in college and after dinner each evening my friends and I would hang out in our dorm rooms and just while away the time having interesting discussions, listening to music or playing cards. So that's what I do now in order to connect to my Divine. It's not something formal. I just know my Divine is with me 24-7 so I invite it in to be with me each and every moment I think to do so. It can be driving, watching a TV show, going to the kitchen to cook, sitting in my hot tub watching the sunrise. Because I'm in conscious contact with Source during each of these moments, those activities become sacred. I carry that attitude with me. The connection made in that moment reflects the sacredness of it.

There's no magic bullet on how this is done. It's your intent and awareness that make it so. Not some ritual with a certain number of prayers and stylized movements you perform because other holy people have prescribed that as the formula for being devout.

The Parable of Your New Neighbor

Let's say a new neighbor moves in next door. You head over and knock on their door, to say hello and meet them.

The next day you go back over and knock on their door. You tell them how much you enjoyed meeting them and let them know you have some leftover pie from your dinner and you brought them a piece.

The next day you again knock on their door. You say you were listening to some music on a streaming service while you were cleaning the garage. You heard an artist you really liked so you downloaded their latest album. You let the neighbor know you brought your music player over with you and ask them if they'd like to listen to the album together.

Every day you go back and knock on your new neighbor's door. Every day you bring them something you thought they'd enjoy, ask them to join you in an activity and shower them with compliments about how pleasant being with them is. You do this every day for three full weeks.

After three weeks, you don't go knock on your neighbor's door. What will your neighbor do?

Your neighbor will wonder why you didn't drop by. And because your neighbor so enjoyed how kind and friendly you were, he or she will want to knock on your door. It could be to check in to see if you're OK, after all, you didn't come by. Or maybe your neighbor simply wants to initiate the contact because she or he enjoyed it so much when you were together.

Do you get the moral of the story? After a short period of reaching out and treating someone like they are your best friend—with no expectations, just expressions of joy from the nature of the connection—that person will respond to you with love and concern. They will begin seeking you out to be in connection with.

What It Looks Like When Your Higher Self Is Your Best Friend

My relationship with my Higher Self changed completely after taking your class. I realized that my Higher Self is my biggest friend! That awareness changed my life. Before I had put it on a pedestal thinking I have to be better, more disciplined, perfect to be even deserving of its Grace and Attention. It is clear to me now it was a bunch of baloney! My Higher Self and I are One. This awareness allows me now to interact all the time with my Higher Self on a daily basis. Every morning I wake up and my first thought is with the purity of my intention to enter the light of my Higher Self, so I can merge as One. Thank you for bringing this awareness to me. It brought an amazing change in my life, changing my identity from an imperfect human to the Bright Spark of Divine Light.

Oksana S.• Fort Pierce, Florida

What a concept, eh? That the Spark of God that you are can be your best friend? It's a long way from the vengeful god who punished those who upset him in the slightest. No offense if you subscribe to the Old Testament teachings of the Western Bible as the be-all and end-all of understanding God. But the God written about in those sacred texts was really unforgiving. He punished the people he liberated from slavery by having them wander around in a desert for forty years—even though that desert was so small you could drive across it in an SUV in two days. He did this because they had a celebration that insulted him by recognizing the Divine in more than just him.

No insecurity in that whole dynamic, nope.

Forgive me for my boldness, but that really doesn't sound like the actions of a God. Love and benevolence are more of what I associate with my God. Those teachings sound a lot more like something written by entities in connection with their lower minds who were more concerned with power and control than a deity who embodies grace and forgiveness.

I'm not here to disparage any religion. If your belief system is working for you, then it's working for you, period—and this book is not for you. But if you're open to expanding your concept of God, I'm happy to encourage you to do so. In the second book of this series, I'll be addressing becoming God-realized. Part of that will be presenting an exercise for you to create your own God, so it will have the perfect attributes for you to fully connect. But for now, I'm simply suggesting you make your Divine your best friend.

The planet is moving out of old, denser 3D energy. Pretty much every institution built from the social, religious, political and economic understandings of the past is going to crumble. The newer, lighter 5D energies of Oneness and benevolence are going to be the foundation from which the Golden Age is built. We're alive at this auspicious time of transition. And this transition will not just be experienced externally. It's a deeply profound shift that will internally affect everyone alive on the planet. And a big, big part of it is letting go of all that separates you from your Source, regardless of how widely practiced such beliefs have been and which holy books proscribe them.

For me, the big shift was about letting go of the unconscious programming that "I am not worthy"—something I kneeled and recited as part of every Catholic Mass my parents took me to.

Consider your Ascension to be a graduation of sorts. You're no longer just a child of God (and all that metaphor implies). You'll begin to recognize yourself as a part of God. As

One with God. Both created by and cocreator with God, because you are that fractal expression of God focused as the consciousness you call yourself. It's wonderful to begin to experience the expansiveness of your true self as you allow yourself to connect to Source in this manner.

The Game Plan

For at least three weeks, constantly talk to your Sacred Higher Self—either aloud or in your head—like it is right next to you. Tell it whatever you are thinking in the moment. Do so in a relational way. Don't just stream of consciousness your thoughts like you do when you're alone. Acknowledge its presence as you're speaking. And constantly invite your Sacred Higher Self to join you in whatever you're doing. Ask it for its opinions as well. Do this even though you probably will not yet be receiving a response. Don't even expect one. Just keep doing it both silently in your imagination and out loud.

For example, when you walk into the kitchen for breakfast you can say, "Higher Self, I've got some cereal in the cupboard and some bacon in the fridge, what do you think would be tasty?" Don't expect an answer. Just ask and invite.

When you're ready to leave for work, consider saying, "Higher Self, I've got a twenty-minute bus ride. Do you want to go with me to keep me company? I can fill you in on the new manager that was just hired." Again, don't expect an answer.

Or when you're at the store trying to choose between two different items of clothing, ask, "Higher Self, I was thinking about the pink one, but I'm not sure how that would look against my skin. Which one do you like?" Do so without expecting an answer.

Do this as often as you can for at least three weeks. Continually invite your Sacred Higher Self into conversation. Ask it to physically be with you. Ask what it thinks about the things you encounter. Don't expect any reply. Just continue to do it.

The reason for not expecting a reply is that your local mind will want to judge your progress. Remember that mind is afraid of losing control. And here you are actively inviting in another voice to give you company and counsel. Your local mind will seize any opportunity it can to reinforce the belief that your efforts are not working, that you should stop this crazy action of talking to something that isn't there. This is why it's important to not expect any replies when you begin to execute this game plan. Just continue to reach out to your Higher Self as often as you can during your daily activities.

Take a guess as to what's going to happen when you reach for connection with your Source many times each day? What did the neighbor in the parable do?

After a while, you're going to start to notice things. It might just be a very tiny sensation at first, so pay attention. What might you notice? Perhaps after you initiate contact you'll feel a tingle. Or maybe feel peaceful. Or perhaps you'll sense a presence.

Celebrate when it happens. Don't feed your doubt by playing into the mind game of trying to determine if something really happened or not. Of course your local mind will tell you it didn't happen. But be honest with yourself. Don't try to understand or explain what happened. Keep it simple. "I felt something." "I kind of noticed something. I'm not sure what, but had a sensation for a brief second." Don't question it. Celebrate it.

Your mind will want to compare what's going on, saying things like, "Other channels say they hear voices." "I hear voices when I talk to someone physically, why don't I hear a voice from Spirit?" Don't go there. When you plant a seed, you may need to water it for a couple of weeks before it sprouts. And when it does first break through the soil, it's tiny. Do you yell at it for not showing up as a fully grown tree when it first appears?

Instead, consider celebrating that the seed you planted has sprouted. Tell yourself, "Goodie! I noticed something. The process is beginning to take root." Then remember the most powerful prayer there is.

Thank you, more please.

Continue the practice of continually speaking to and inviting your best friend to be with you, but now begin doing so with the awareness that sometimes, you are noticing a response of some sort. Don't expect one. Just notice when it happens, no matter how small it is. And then be grateful.

Thank you, more please.

Over time, you'll become frequently aware of physical sensations, a sense of presence, and maybe you'll even hear something. Just continue on with gratitude until your awareness of this kind of connection happens daily. Then it's time to up your game.

Tell you're Sacred Higher Self that you're so excited about the connection that has been established. Let it know that you'd like to be able to understand it better. This is the time to ask for responses in ways you can understand.

Once again, you'll need to stay open to how Spirit may respond to you. Have you ever heard of the Clairs? They're six psychic senses various mediums commonly have developed.

- Clairaudience – Hearing sounds clearly, as if someone is speaking to you

- Clairvoyance – Seeing visions of the past, present, future or other possible timelines

- Claircognizance – Instantly knowing things

- Clairsentience – Feeling the energies and emotions of people and spirits around you

- Clairalience – Smelling odors that have no physical

source

- Clairgustance – Tasting something that you are not physically eating

Your Higher Self will respond to you in ways you can accept. Maybe you have a predilection for one of these abilities because of your current life interests or your past life experiences. However Spirit responds, don't force it. Allow what is being given to come to you. Just continue to acknowledge, with gratitude, that you are receiving something, and allow it to unfold.

In my case, I get energy squirts. Yup, clair-energence is a thing. I feel/sense a bunch of energy when I'm channeling. That's it. There're no words coming to me. My game is played by trying to make sense of what message is contained in that energy. Early on I've learned to practice discernment. I focused on developing my sense of when something "feels" true. I use that feeling to guide my understanding of the messages I receive. Thus when I channel, it sounds like I'm talking, because I am. I'm giving words to what I'm energetically sensing.

As I've practiced doing this, it has become much quicker, easier, and clear. Even in writing this book, I simply let the energetics of thoughts Spirit sends me from the thought sphere come to mind, and then flesh them out as best I can using my vocabulary. I can sense when I've jumped off track. If something doesn't feel right, I go back and rewrite that section. If what I write feels good, then I "know" I've interpreted the guidance correctly.

Source tells me that each of us can access all the Clairs, but it will be more in alignment with your nature to let yours emerge naturally in whatever order they show up. You can force the issue and choose one to develop, but doing so will bypass some of the trust and connection your Divine wishes to have with you. So let it come as it may. Your Sacred Higher Self knows you want to connect with it, so it will arrange for it to happen in the best possible way for you once you start actively taking steps to move toward it.

For me, this means accepting that for the most part, my abilities at this time are to interpret energy squirts. Yours could be automatic writing. Divining through tea leaves, dowsing rods or pendulums. If you're drawn to it, then it's for you. That's how it works in 5D. We're really only shown the next step to take, not the entire route that will be mapped out.

> *I feel driven to expand my spiritual consciousness and Peter's course provided valuable building blocks in my quest for growth. I learned that emotional blocks are the main reason why I'm not experiencing 5D living. Peter taught us practical techniques to remove these blocks ... [These] methods work fantastically by the way! Additionally I was pleased to learn that it is possible to connect with angels and enlightened beings; that I can request and expect miracles and that spiritual skills can*

be shared simply by being open to this possibility. And yes, I do talk to my Higher Self regularly now and my life is filled with miracles.

Ana Maria Scott • Nice, France

Are You Ready to Channel?

If you can speak with your Higher Self, you can speak with any conscious entity. It's just a matter of frequency. If you know the frequency (energy signature or name) of a consciousness, you can communicate with it.

Consider FM radio. There're lots and lots of stations broadcasting in your area. And when you tune in your receiver to the frequency of a particular station, you can listen to it. All the other stations haven't gone away. They're still broadcasting, it's just you've tuned in to one particular one and so that's the one you can hear.

If you have not yet realized it, prepare to be blown away. You're swimming in a sea of conscious life.

There are countless entities (i.e., other fractals of God) all in the field of Oneness along with yourself. We haven't been aware of this, because before we did not have the ability to tune in. But to continue the FM radio example, just because you don't have a radio receiver, it doesn't mean there's no one out there broadcasting.

I was shocked when I was first aware of how much conscious life exists and how much of it is eager to communicate. You see, every time I channel a message, I'm flooded with profound joy. Just the act of making that connection is, in and of itself, pleasurable—you know that bliss I keep telling you that you are. Connecting to Spirit immediately puts me in a state of physically feeling it. This is pretty much the reason why so many other conscious entities seek out communication. It feels so good when it takes place.

On my final trip to Oneness University, I had a very special experience of touching a ball of solid gold about the size of a basketball. This ball was kept in a very sacred chamber, with enlightened monks chanting prays over it twenty-four hours a day. They were creating a physical place for Source itself, in the form of golden light, to reside in 3D. I fell to my knees the moment I was allowed to touch it, and then slept for some time afterward. When I awoke, the largest shames I have lived with my whole life were gone. Simply gone.

I could still remember what happened and the actions I took that I carried such shame over, but all the emotional blockages holding that shame in place were no longer with me. This amazing release of such powerful trapped emotions opened me up in a big, big way. I could suddenly hear countless entities all around me. It was like I had gone from a quiet library straight into a rock concert!

When I returned home, I asked a mentor about it. He told me to tell them to shut up. I did.

And it worked. I was back to the quiet existence I had before I touched the Golden Ball. The problem was that I threw out the baby with the bathwater. I set back my channeling abilities by almost a decade because I declared to the Universe I didn't want to hear it. And of course, because I have free will and I'm sovereign, that's exactly what happened.

In *My Ascension Handbook – Level II*, the next book in this series, I will provide you more detailed instructions on how to channel. For now I simply want to tell you that if you can speak with your Sacred Higher Self, you can speak with any entity you can identify. For now I'd like to give you the basic directions for ensuring you're not overwhelmed by so many connections and that you connect only with entities of your choice.

Setting Your Boundaries

First and foremost, understand you are sovereign. You are literally the master of your consciousness and all that comes into it. Remember how I suggested that your Ascension will be like a graduation? Here's your diploma. It's a statement declaring you are sovereign.

Nothing, absolutely nothing, can come into my consciousness without my permission.

This is a fact. If you find there's anything in your sphere of being that you're not happy about, it's time to own up to being a powerful creator. Own up to the fact that on some unconscious level you've invited that into your life. Now do you get why the entire second step presented in this book is about cleaning up your unconscious by releasing the blocked energies held there?

So are you ready to graduate? Are you ready to leave your childhood behind where God is your parent who sets up rules you have to follow or you'll be punished? Are you ready to step up to the magnificence of being a part of God, and claim all the power that implies?

It means you stop being a victim. I'm not saying you ignore or bypass any of the pains you've experienced that were caused by others. Not at all. That's what the entire second step is about—taking responsibility all that pain by fully feeling and expressing it. And having done this, are you willing to stop telling the story of being a victim? Are you willing to see how you held attractive energy that brought even more of those pains to you? And now that you've released them, are you willing to choose new energies that draw to you all the treasures of Divinity—the keys to the kingdom, so to speak? Are you willing to own that because you're a fractal of God, you're the creator of your own experience?

Remember how I've hinted over and over that when you complete an experience by fully feeling it, you gain wisdom? Well, this is the wisdom I've been talking about. It was you all along who created that experience. And when you own that you've done so, you can move on to creating new, better experiences. And the super cool part is that you're not doing it alone. It's you and Source, doing it hand in hand.

I'd like to address fear, as it's a subtly corrosive energy that works to prevent you from claiming your Divinity. I know many people who are able to channel and interact in 5D realms. And many of them are afraid. They have all kinds of "protection" rituals to keep all the "bad" entities at bay. Guess what? They're inviting the very entities they are afraid of into their consciousness by using all their wards to keep them out.

I'm not saying there are not "bad" entities. It's kind of like 3D people. Some are kind and loving, and some are not. Some 4D entities take advantage when they can. When we get to the section on discernment in the next book, you'll have tools to detect people and entities with those kinds of denser energies and simply step away from them. But for now, here's a blanket technique to allow only that which you choose to come to you. Declare you are sovereign. Shout it from the rooftops.

I AM SOVEREIGN!

Declare aloud a declaration of yourself as being sovereign. Say it as if it is THE LAW. Because it is.

Respect your sovereign declaration like it's the Constitution, the Magna Carta and the Ten Commandments all rolled into one.

Remember, nothing can come into your consciousness without your permission. Acknowledge that you, and only you, are the determiner of what comes to you. Then own the consequences of your actions.

During the recent health scare around COVID, many people started sovereignty movements as a response to government forays attacking health freedom. It was interesting for me to see people who on one hand would claim to be sovereign, and then in the very next breath say something like, "They make me wear a mask," or "They won't let me fly unless I …"

The reality is that no one can make you do anything. People can prevent you from doing some things you may prefer to do, like be on a plane while you are unmasked. But no one made you get on that plane or put on that mask. That's why I'm saying be prepared to own the consequences of your actions. Because when you do, you'll find all kinds of unconscious beliefs and trapped emotions triggering experiences for you to (hopefully) clear. And as you do clear those, you become truly free. You live your sovereignty by making your choices and reaping the benefits of how those choices bring people and experiences to you.

Claiming your sovereignty as it relates to channeling means you get to set the ground rules for interactions with all nonphysical entities. Here're the rules I use:

> 1. Only entities in conscious service to Divine love are allowed to interact with me. All other entities may not

come into my sphere of consciousness at all.

2. Any entity that wishes to communicate with me must ask my permission. This means they first wait to get my attention and say hello and ask if I'd like to communicate before any energy or messages are transmitted.

3. Any entity that does speak with me must tell me its name, that is, give me full access to their energetic frequency without concealing any information about themselves.

These requirements keep all my interactions super clean. There's never ulterior motives or deception. I'm not bothered by having too many contacts. And any contact that does take place is carried out with love and respect.

Did you notice how this set of ground rules keeps out all the entities that other people call "bad?" And it does so without having to perform any rituals or set any wards? Instead of acting from fear, these ground rules announce and allow only love. There's no dissolution of your focus by trying to judge or condemn others for their actions. It's all about you owning your power through pronouncing it.

Declare your ground rules for contact aloud to put them into effect. Speak them like you're an action hero saying their catchphrase after you've just defeated the villains and saved the day. Say it like you're the judge and you just dropped the gavel. Say it until you believe it, that is, until you no longer have unconscious charges arise that trigger you because of your declaration.

Remember, if you have any resistance come up in you, it's probably another trapped emotion that's showing up because you're ready to clear it. Use what you learned in step 2 and then continue declaring your sovereignty and speaking aloud your ground rules until they feel true.

Notice how this is done from a place of owning and claiming your power. I never go into the manifestation of other people's fears because I never invite them in. If you're casting spells to protect yourself, then on some level you believe there are bad things out there that you need to be protected from. It's that unconscious belief that will then generate the attractive pull of those "bad" people and outcomes you're fearful of.

If you understand what is presented here, you'll only have the tremendous nonphysical interactions you desire. Rather than turn everything off by telling them all to shut up, I've learned to set it up so that it's relatively quiet in my head. If I want to speak to an entity, I do so. I give them the same courtesy that I've asked for. I locate them by focusing on their frequency (name), and then say hello. Then I ask if they'd like to converse.

Some consciousnesses do continue to seek me out. And it's always because our interests match and they're excited to connect and share about it. Take the connection I had with Mira. She sought me out because she's looking for humans whose energetic fields are broadcasting they are ready to embrace more of their 5D skills. She explained to me that she's part of the first wave that's preparing humanity for physical contact with our star brothers and sisters. She took joy in helping me grow, and I took joy in growing. She modeled that connection to me, so that as my skills developed, I would be able to declare my sovereignty and set up the ground rules that allow for only these types of interactions to take place.

Allow me to close this chapter by stating what has hopefully become obvious to you after reading this far. You use the same skills to communicate directly with your Higher Self to speak to any other entity that has the ability to move their awareness into 4 or 5D. It's all open to you. ETs. Inner Earth folk. Angels. Plant and animal kingdoms. They are all other manifestations of the Oneness you'll know as your consciousness allows. It's all real and available.

Even though I really want you to buy my next book, don't wait until it's available before you begin to claim your universal citizenship. Call on Mira from the Pleiades for help. Go ahead and talk to Archangel Michael—he's told me he'd be happy to receive you. If you read or listen to another channeler speak to a consciousness that intrigues you, make the connection. Although I'll be offering more practical suggestions to fine-tune your abilities, why wait?

One day, one of my skeptical conservative Christian relatives wanted to know a bit more about my channeling abilities. I asked her if she spoke with Jesus. She said she did. I asked if

Jesus spoke back. She said he did. I told her that's great! She has a personal, clear connection with the Divine as expressed through her understanding of Christ consciousness. I told her that's exactly what I do. Except I talk to more than just Christ.

Living An Ascended Life

If you're waiting for things to become night-and-day different because you completed Level I of your Ascension, don't hold your breath.

First off, "Level I" is just an arbitrary marker I've set so that the information in this series of handbooks is easier to ingest. There's no particular point at which you're ascended or not. One moment you can be all spacious and connected with 5D energy, and the next you can be singularly focused on that 3D jerk who cut you off in traffic. Ascension is not an absolute. It's more about your ability to move your consciousness up and down the density ladder, so to speak.

And this is a good thing. For the most part, those of us who have begun our Ascension journeys are living in 4D. We have one foot in 3D and one foot in 5D. The game is about mastering this level of density. At the lower end of the spectrum, it means doing your best to practice awareness when you find yourself reacting rather than responding to your experiences. At the higher end it means appreciating the miracles coming to you by knowing you've cocreated them. You allowed yourself to receive them. And you're grateful for them, often expressed both in words and sharing your blessings with others.

The more you keep your focus on mastering the moment you're in, the more you'll be elevating your consciousness to 5D frequencies. And when you become aware that, "Oops, I did whatever behavior I'm judging again," you use the opportunity created by your awareness to process whatever lower-density energies you've tuned into. It's your chance to complete that experience and gain its wisdom. It's how both you and everyone on the planet evolves.

Don't think for a moment that you're in this alone. Every little bit of dense energy you transmute lightens the entire field of the Earth plane. Everyone benefits from your act of heavy lifting, just as you benefit from all of theirs.

That's why I spoke earlier about how Awakening and Ascension are inevitable. We've passed the field energy thresholds that simply will not allow third density energies to dictate mass experience in the ways they have in the past. Please join me in a big THANK YOU to all the Consciousness in creation that moved us to the point where we get the honor of being in the first wave of mass Ascension.

But just because our Ascension is inevitable, it doesn't mean it's time to just kick back and chill (except for a few well-deserved vacations every year—lol). On a societal level, do you want this transition to take up to twenty generations before everyone enjoys the ease and grace of living in 5D most of the time? Do you really want all the wars and political and religious divisions to fester for decades before enough of us choose to no longer allow such density into the planetary field?

On a personal level, do you want to have to go through dying of old age and disease and then reincarnate once more without full memory of your true self? Or would you rather consciously choose when and how you transition from your body to your soul, choosing while you're alive now if you'll be coming back and who you'll be coming back as so you can continue to build the dreams you're working to manifest for the Earth?

This is one of the choices Ascension presents us. I'm choosing quick and easy as my Ascension path. And if it means that from time to time I will feel intensely the suffering that I've denied for so long from my experience, I say, "Bring it on!"

Sure, I can complain about all the rigors of working toward my goal. I can even indulge in the fear of doubt that this isn't even real, and even if it is, it's not really happening for me. In fact, I still react in both these ways to experiences I have. But just as I told you that Ascension allows your consciousness to move up and down densities, I know that at any moment I can change my course and get back on the track of growth I prefer. And the more times I'm able to shift the focus of my consciousness in my preferred way, the quicker and easier it becomes. And the sooner the miracles I pray for begin to manifest in my life.

It truly is a path of ease and grace, even though it doesn't seem like it at times. Yes, I still worry about money from time to time. And yes, I'm truly abundant and provided with everything I desire whenever I allow myself to receive it.

Sounds like a conundrum, doesn't it? Welcome to 4D, the transitional place where we can sort out the dance of densities. So let go of the idea that everything is peaches and cream and tacos and salsa now because you've ascended. The learning and growth never stop. But for the most part, the hard stuff is over and we'll continue our growth from a platform of greater ease and grace. For me, nothing in my life has been more satisfying. That's why I'm thrilled to share these steps with you. Writing this book is like being honored to host a giant "Welcome to the Golden Age" party!

Let's begin by exploring some simple practices to help you live an ascended life.

Laugh

And when you're done laughing, play. And then laugh some more.

Part of the grind of 3D was everyone buying into the debt slavery system we allowed power mongers to impose on us. You know, the getting up and going to work every day that most schooling trained us to accept. And the fear that comes with never seeming to have enough. Or the self-loathing promoted by media systems that tell you how much you suck because you don't own this product or live that lifestyle. These are some pretty dense energies we're releasing ourselves from. And we've been conditioned to take it all so seriously. Our compassion has been used against us by those who seek control. We all want things to be better, but we've been trained to stay in the lower frequencies of worrying about what the problem is, rather than envisioning with gratitude the manifestation of what we want.

If you need to, please go back and reread the part in step 1 about how to pray. The action of giving your attention to the societal problems you worry about actually props up the energetic frequencies allowing those problems to exist. The solution isn't to fix things in 3D. It's to open up your vibrational field to higher density frequencies and then fixing that reality in your consciousness so that it becomes grounded on the planet. By doing so you will become an amplifier and transmitter of those lighter frequencies that uplift the world. The slime simply oozes off the walls because there's no longer anything there for it to stick to.

So laugh!

Every time you laugh you automatically put yourself on a lighter frequency. Make it a regular habit until you find yourself laughing constantly throughout your day regardless of what external circumstances you may be experiencing.

If you're like me, your laugh muscles will have been pretty much atrophied by the time you realize how important laughter is to Ascension. I had to spend some time practicing laughter simply to reopen the ability in me.

It's not hard to practice. Look up Laughter Yoga videos on YouTube. Or better yet, join a live Laughter Yoga group that meets regularly. And you have probably watched at least one TV show sometime in your life that made you laugh. Subscribe to a streaming service and make it a daily practice to watch an episode a day of something you find funny. Keep at it even if it seems stupid and you're not laughing. It will only be a matter of time before you reconnect with the joy you remembered and start laughing regularly again.

This practice may not seem very important, but it is. Laughing regularly is training and conditioning your physical and emotional bodies to attune to a lighter frequency. That's why some people have been able to cure terminal diseases simply by watching programs that made them laugh.

What do you have to lose by trying this? Your sour disposition?

As you begin to laugh more and more, you're going to notice that lots of things around you will change for your benefit. Simply by inducing a higher frequency through laughter, you will attract more and more of what you do want and less and less of all that stuff you've been worrying about. Your consciousness won't be able to hold all the lower-density thoughts localized mind has been feeding you. You'll naturally feel lighter. And you'll laugh more and more and more!

Work Less, Allow More

Where intent meant so much in 3D, allowance means more in 5D.

We spoke of how the 3D economy is rigged so that you're always working but always behind. An insidious part of its design is to keep you tired. When you're working so hard just to get by, then you'll naturally going to rest whenever you get the chance. And since all the Ascension steps outlined in this book require some effort on your part, the more you're working the less you'll be Ascending.

Solution, work less.

What! Work less?

Yup. We're moving into a density where things that take effort won't even feel like work. Your activities will be fueled by joy and connection, because that is the currency that matters in 5D. Now I'm not saying quit your job. Do whatever you need to do to feel comfortable. But as you do, be sure to practice step 1 so you'll Awaken. Awakening will allow you to work more efficiently when you are working.

Then consider letting go of the things that fill your schedule. If something you're doing doesn't bring you joy, don't do it. Later we'll talk more about how claiming your power makes you sovereign. Start by setting very clear boundaries with your time and effort. Contemplate anything you're doing that doesn't bring you joy. See if there's an unconscious belief or trapped emotion you're compensating for by doing that those things. Beliefs like, "If I just succeed my parents will love me," are often at the root of a workaholic's obsession. Once you've identified your unconscious motivation for doing things that don't give you joy, process it as explained in step 2.

When you do you'll find that you begin to receive more of what you've been unconsciously working so hard to achieve. You'll no longer be attracting the experience of what you've lacked (including money), and begin attracting more of what you desire. You know, the things that bring you joy.

Lots of people have lamented that the world economy has displaced so many workers. And many feel bad that COVID measures shuttered so many businesses. Not me. Like it or not, these outcomes have given hundreds of millions of people a pause. They were suddenly forced to take time off. And many are choosing to use that time to first recover from exhaustion, and then to go inward and begin allowing the Ascension energies to take root on the planet. Have you ever wondered why so many people never rushed back to work once things opened up? Part of it is so many of us tasted what it's like to be more free. We realized that even though money may be tight, we're living our lives just fine and are much happier as a result.

Find ways to work less. Let go of anything you're doing that doesn't bring you joy. Process any fears that arise along the way. And then practice allowing what you previously worked for to come to you naturally. Remember Step 3 – Inviting Your Sacred Higher Self Into Your Life. As you connect more and more with your Source, you'll naturally feel safer and more supported. As you allow the benevolence of the Divine to come to you by opening space for it to do so (both energetically by clearing blockages and physically by working less), you'll begin to receive more fulfillment on all levels, including financial. And over time, you'll come to believe this is the way the world truly works when you ascend, instead of buying into false programs like the only things you can count on are death and taxes.

And while you're pondering how to work less, be sure to include working less at your ascension as well. Transitioning can be really stressful. Our bodies are changing on an energetic and cellular level. You're going to need lots of time to rest and relax. Build that into your ascension plan. Spending an hour a day is a lot of time to really focus on ascending. Make sure you're spending the other twenty-three hours of the day taking care of yourself and doing what brings you joy.

I can't recommend enough for you to go out into nature. Every day if you can. Even if it's nothing more than a small park in your neighborhood. Step out of your day-to-day existence and commune with nature. As your abilities to speak with conscious entities take hold, practice talking to Gaia. Mother Earth has a lot of wisdom and love to share. Let yourself receive it regularly and bask in the restorative energies She provides in nature settings.

Here's a fun incident for you to ponder as you consider allowing more. During a recent meditation circle a participant said he received a message from Spirit telling him to stop trying and start allowing. We all laughed when he said his mind turned that into "I should try to allow."

Let Go of Attending to Problems in the World

I hitchhiked a lot when I was in college. About seventeen thousand miles all told. I wasn't aware of it at the time, but I was in flow when I hitched. I just thought I was naturally lucky. It never took me more than a few minutes to get a ride. Nearly every trip I ended up with someone dropping me off at the doorstep of where I was headed. I timed my trips and always traveled faster than a bus line would cover that same route. And I usually ended up with more money in my pocket than when I started because so many good natured people were so generous.

It was easy—until it wasn't. On one trip, I spent three hours in an underpass, hiding from the sun, waiting for a ride. I had never before encountered difficulty like this getting a ride. I was angry. Hurt. Bored. Wondering if I was OK. The underpass smelled terrible. It was dirty. Nasty.

Then out of the corner of my eye, I spied a tiny flower sprouting up next to an oil slick, with a rainbow of light reflecting on it. I thought to myself, that's really pretty. A ride instantly stopped to pick me up.

What happened under that underpass was an important lesson for me. Even though I was worried and uncomfortable, even though I was surrounded by filth and stench, the moment I allowed my awareness to find beauty in the situation, everything shifted. I was back in the flow of instant rides.

I'd like you to consider if you're choosing to live under a dirty, smelly underpass.

You see, all the dehumanizing structures built during the Kali Yuga are crumbling. The truth is, from a 3D point of view, it's going to appear to get worse before it gets better. The corruption has always been there, but now the veils are being lifted so we're going to see how horrible things have become before enough momentum is built to change them—at least on the 3D level.

But in 5D, the timeline of Shangri La exists right next to the timeline of all the Earth's problems being pushed into our awareness by the media (and alternative media) systems.

It's just a matter of being aware such a heavenly existence is possible, clearing the blockages that keep you energetically stuck outside it, then allow it to come to you by putting your focus there.

If you're still attending to popular media systems, then, sorry for you!

Stop it.

You're allowing your attention to be directed to all that's wrong. I know lots of spiritual people who still feed themselves a diet of news and then from time to time have outbursts of hatred toward whoever is being demonized at the moment. At the time of this publication in 2023, the major focus of media-generated hatred is either Donald Trump or Joe Biden, depending on whether you choose to give your attention to mainstream media or alternative media. And since the debris from the collapse of the 3D energy systems that support the mass media may take a while to dissipate, don't be surprised as new boogey people are coronated every few years.

Now of course, there's lots broken in the world that we'd all like to fix. But if there's one bit of wisdom I can give you to help live in 5D it's that you don't kill a dragon by slaying it. It only loses its power over you when you love it. If you find you have hatred, or any attachment at all, to someone because of the bad things they're doing, understand how they're a mirror. They're showing you something that is wrong, hence your feeling of discomfort. And the wrong they're showing you isn't just their doing. It's also a part of you. On some level you've allowed it or you would not be experiencing it in your field with the discomfort you have.

Your feelings about those bad people won't go away by you killing them or bringing them to justice. It's an inside job. The disgust you feel for them is a reflection of the unconscious disgust you have for that emotion itself. You've attracted that experience to complete it, not to punish it or send it away. You have to love yourself for having that experience and emotional response. You have to love the emotion enough to allow it to express itself no matter how wrong or bad it feels. When you do, you'll naturally feel forgiveness for the perpetrators of the actions that triggered you. You will have loved the dragon that is both inside you and embodied externally by the person you're hating on. And because you loved it, the dragon will have lost its power. You're now free to attract and experience more of what brings you joy.

If you're called to take action in the 3D world, by all means you should do so. My plea is that you do so consciously. Have you contemplated why you're so drawn to this tragedy that you feel compelled to rectify? Is there an unconscious belief or a trapped emotion of your own pain and suffering that's driving you? And can you fully feel that internally before you try to fix it externally?

There's lots to worry about if you let yourself. Evil ETs controlling things. AI. The Cabal. The destruction of the environment. And lots more. Can you love it enough (or love yourself enough) to really feel what's being triggered in you by giving your full attention and permission to express the emotion you have around it?

You can start by being aware of when you're disaster-bating! You know, telling everyone you meet about all the terrible things you have learned. In addition to recommending you stop attending to news, please stop putting yourself in the low-energy frequency of getting together with like-minded folks so you can obsessively tell each other the latest "inside intel" on the most recent terrible plot being perpetrated to enslave humanity.

It's one thing to have an awareness of an external ill and use that as impetus to find your attraction to it internally, but it's a whole other banana for you to gain significance by letting everyone around you know how perceptive you are for seeing what's going on, how you've seen through the illusions and know the secret reasons why and how all these travesties are taking place. I urge you to choose instead to process the charges your awareness has raised. When you do, you'll no longer try to fill the void within you by participating in that select society of smart people playing the "truther" game.

The folks who are busy disaster-bating don't realize they're playing the exact role the power mongers desire of them. The "evil" people who have run things in 3D aren't stupid. They're more aware of how 4D energy works than most. They are just cut off from Source and are trying to fill that void with feelings of power and control. And all the supposedly awake people obsessed with the truth movement are playing into the power mongers' hands. The more you hold your focus on the 3D problems, the more you permission the energy that allows those problems to take place.

Once you become aware of a travesty, feel your feelings about it. Then say NO to it. Make a statement out loud that you do not give permission for that to be on your planet. This is an important step toward pulling your unconscious energetic power away from fueling whatever you see as being a problem.

Then once you've said no to something, let it go. Don't keep feeding it with your attention and worry. Focus on what you want, not what you don't want. Your focus pretty much determines the experience you'll have in the lighter energies of 5D.

Remember when I asked you to claim your sovereignty by first understanding that nothing, absolutely nothing can come into your field without your permission? What do you think takes place when you get together with others and focus your connection on sharing information about problems? Or leading the charge to fight for justice to be enacted around those problems?

You create more problems. You give them permission to come to you because you react from a place of victimhood: "Look at all the bad things those evil people are doing!" Your focus on things that engender fear gives life to that fear.

Stop focusing on it. Once you're aware something is out of kilter, contemplate it. Ask your Sacred Higher Self about it, about why you're attracted to it. Then complete the experience by fully feeling the emotions attached to it. Don't keep recreating the pain by only mentally dwelling on it or physically fighting to change it. Love the dragon.

It will be the collective effect of enough of us holding our focus on the beneficence of 5D that will create a field strong enough to move the entire planet out of any darker timelines you may be worried about. I know this will happen. I'm sharing my hope with you so that together there will be much less stuck energy being recycled that is creating the resistance to the timeline shift for everyone's betterment right now.

And in the newer, lighter energies of 5D, we'll all be able to build the structures that give us joy—things like an abundance economy, and a food system that is both nourishing and respectful of nature. If you can imagine it, it's possible. Do your best to imagine and create what you desire instead of fighting against that which you despise.

The change to Earth living on a more benevolent timeline can happen as quickly as we allow it. If you're being called to take action for the betterment of all, I ask for your help in the great work of giving your power to the visions of paradise you desire. And once you do your internal work, don't be surprised if everything you do externally becomes more fruitful.

Find Your Tribe

Recall how I explained earlier that localized mind tries to keep control by separating you from your experiences? Basically, local mind is telling you stories. It tells them over and over again. And enough people have shared the stories of their minds disguised as great works of philosophy or spiritually so that the stories glorifying mind permeate everything we've learned about the world and everything most of us do. Are you ready to tell a different story?

It's a story about how powerful you are, because you were born as a spark of God. It's a story of the limitless you. A you that is consciousness, existence, bliss. It's the story of how you awoke, not just to seeing the ills in the world, but to the understanding that you are the creator of that reality. The story of how you realized that nothing can come into your field of being without your permission.

As you claim your power, you'll stop telling the story of being a victim to the whims of the world around you and start telling the story of the powerful God Source Energy Being you are.

Be aware as you tell your story. Consider what it's about. Is it a history of all that has "happened" to you? Or is it a story about the dreamscape you're entering into because you know the truth about yourself and you know how the story ends—we all ascend and merge with God.

I know these last few paragraphs sound like pie in the sky, fanciful thinking.

Exactly! It's your story, so how do you want to tell it?

At first most people living an ascended life were reluctant to tell the story of their truth. Friends don't understand it. Family thinks we're crazy when we drop hints about Spirituality that is not couched in terms of the religion we were raised with. That's why it important that you find your tribe.

To fully embrace being the ascended person you're becoming, you'll need to be able to speak freely about you transformation. You'll need at least a few close friends who won't worry about you when you start sharing what seems fancifully amazing to most people. You need a tribe.

Finding a tribe is an important bit of advice Spirit asked me to pass along to the majority of people I've worked with individually as an ascension coach. It's hard enough dealing with all the ascension symptom our bodies are experiencing as it moves from being carbon based to crystalline. That's why I prescribed lots of rest earlier. Aches, pains, headaches, sleeplessness are all ascension symptoms. Your body needs time to adjust and recover from its growth. That's hard enough to do. But having to deal with loneliness and ridicule also takes a toll.

Finding a tribe gives you a group of friends who understand. It gives you a place where you can relax, share experiences and hope. It allows you to laugh together about your growth. Pray together. Give and receive support. Your tribe is your Spiritual home.

Nearly everyone I've given this advice to had no idea where to look to find their tribe, let alone the wherewithal to start their own. To help, my wife and I created an online tribe you can join – The Becoming Awesome Community. It's a home for people who've embraced ascension as central to their lives.

We meet online, live, weekly so we can look someone in the eyes as we share and then meditate together to deepen our connections. Over time the weekly meetups will form into a group consciousness allowing everyone to benefit from the strength of group prayer. The Becoming Awesome Community also has a 24/7 chat server dedicated to it for whenever you feel a desire to connect. Finding your own tribe or joining the Becoming Awesome Community reminds you you're not alone, even though you local mind will try to tell you that you are. Connecting with others going through their own ascension changes will help quell the doubts your local mind raises. And having the courage to speak your own story will be big leap for you personally.

The Becoming Awesome Community is built around the patreon platform with a small monthly fee. You can go to Patreon.com and search for Becoming Awesome or follow this link to join: https://www.patreon.com/BecomingAwesome

One of the greatest miracles my wife and I have been blessed with is the group consciousness we formed through our weekly meditation circle that we've hosted since 2011. Now we have the power of the Angels, Guides and Higher Selves of our entire circle joining with us whenever we pray, even when we do so alone. And check this amazing benefit - whenever one person in our group has a leap of growth or develops a new 5D skill, we all get it. The person who first receives that blessing shares their experience and then we all focus on receiving it during our weekly meetup. Since our consciousness is linked, it's easy. Low and behold, those 5D abilities and expanded consciousness soon become ours. It's an incredible gift that's accelerated our growth. That's why I'm so excited about the Becoming Awesome Community. Everyone in it will have an accelerated path into ascension!

Another outlet for sharing ascension stories is the Becoming Awesome series Tracy and I have produced for Gnostic TV. Each episode has a an ordinary person sharing how 5D abilities work in their everyday life. Then we use our connection to Source to transmit activations for those 5D abilities to viewers. Hearing about these abilities creates a framework for your mind to allow its possibility for you. We then instruct viewers on how to get into a Oneness Field with us and our guests. While in this field, we transmit the energetic blueprint for people ready to allow that ability to manifest in their own lives. In the first season we had shows to activate Light Language, tap into Medical Intuition, Automatic Knowing, Uniting with Your Future Self, Receiving Angelic Guidance, Benefitting from Sacred Geometry, Allowing and Animal Communication. Of course, the more clearing work you've done and the quieter your mind has become, the more you'll be ready to start manifesting 5D abilities in your own life. It goes back to the analogy of preparing the soil before you plant the seeds. But when you are ready to allow 5D skills to begin manifesting for you, this program can e a great help.

When you feel ready to view the Becoming Awesome 5D activation series, please use this link to subscribe to Gnostic TV from your computer or handheld device. Using this link ensures a portion of your subscription fee is returned to Tracy & I for producing the program: https://tinyurl.com/becomingawesome

We know that many people are ready to begin expressing 5D skills and are using their own 5D abilities. That's why we've produced the Becoming Awesome TV series. But truth be told, your ascension is more about what you allow for yourself than what others, even Spirit, gives to you. And belonging to a tribe gives you a place where allowing a 5D lifestyle to unfold is natural and supported. You can share the truth of who you are and be loved and welcomed for it. That's the true test of living an ascended life.

You see, you don't get a diploma on a piece of paper when you graduate to 5D. No one else can tell you that you've arrived. Asserting your own inner authority is the sign your consciousness is aligned with 5D. Your diploma is the energetic act of you claiming you've arrived. At the heart of all the steps I've outlined in this book is the awareness that everything is yours when you claim and allow it. You put your awareness on what you desire. You do so with gratitude that it has already manifested, because you know that in the vastness of creation, there is a timeline where this is true.

You then identify any blockages you hold that keep you from enjoying your preferred timeline. You own those blockages. You contemplate them and clear them by allowing their full expression.

As you do so, you'll feel more and more connected to Spirit, to Source. You'll begin to communicate directly with it. You'll feel the love of benevolence permeating the field of creation itself.

Now you're ready to take the next step in your Ascension. Claim your power. Claim your seat in the Kingdom of Heaven. From there you entered into cocreation with God itself. God didn't make you to be small. God gave you access to the powers of creation. Ascension is simply the realization that you've received this gift..

Claim your power. Give yourself your diploma. Do your best to think and act as if you're already ascended. And then enjoy the ride as the awe, mystery and essence of the Divine field of which you are a part reveals itself to you in ever more wondrous ways.

You are blessed! Live like it.

Peter's Bio

I received a PhD from Penn State in 1992. I taught media literacy for decades and authored the Alcohol Literacy Challenge™, the world's first evidence-based youth alcohol prevention curricula proven in eight research studies to reduce underage and binge drinking in a single ninety-minute session.

Living in Guam just before 1990, I began my spiritual growth while practicing recovery in a twelve-step program. I also seriously practiced moving stuck emotional charges that were in me by reading all seven books in the *Right Use of Will* series by Ceanne DeRohan, allowing myself to be triggered as I read.

After moving to Santa Fe, New Mexico, in 1995, I studied and practiced teachings from Kryon who is channeled through Lee Carroll, and Abraham who is channeled through Ester Hicks.

I took my first class in how to become a channel shortly after 2000 with Spiritualist Pastor Drew Vogt.

During the mid-2000s I attended beginner and Blue College classes at the Ramtha School of Enlightenment. Ramtha is channeled by J. Z. Knight.

In the early 2010s I took four, month-long trips to India to study at Oneness University, founded by the avatar Sri Bhagavan. During this time I became a Oneness Trainer and was given the gift of Awakening. Over the next several years I taught dozens of Oneness classes and organized large Oneness Meditations that passed along the energies of Awakening to thousands of New Mexicans.

I moved in with my beloved, Tracy Juechter, and together we have been hosting a weekly meditation circle since 2011, one that is still ongoing. In 2019 this circle formed into a group consciousness we call Elan, using the Info-Looping technique discovered by GW Hardin.

To celebrate the dawn of the Golden Age, I traveled to an event in Colorado that hosted a stop on the 11.11.11 Crystal Skulls World Mysteries tour organized by a Central American shaman seeking to help unite the Eagle and Condor (the spiritual energies of the North and the South). While there I touched a five thousand year old crystal skull and dropped to the ground. When I came around, the skull's keeper told me I had received a download and that the information I received would unfold over time—which Spirit tells me is why my channeling abilities took off to new heights when I went to Egypt in 2022.

In 2013, while on a tour of Machu Picchu and Lake Titicaca with Lee Carroll, I became aware of a portal near the Sunken Temple at Tiwanaku in Bolivia. There I established contact with a group of Pleiadians who offered information whenever I chose to connect, though I did not appreciate the magnitude of this gift at the time and rarely used it until 2020.

In the mid-2010s I was asked to speak at a Children of the Light conference in Denver about giving Oneness Deeksha (energetic blessings for Awakening). While there I was initiated to transmit the energy of the Wholeness Blessing that was sourced from Archangel Michael. It was at this conference that I met GW. I studied with GW during the late 2010s, learning how to implement the science and math behind his discoveries of Inherent Thriving, Info-Looping, the Gatekeeper Effect, and Allowing the Experience of Essence, Radiance and Mystery through Time-Space.

I have taken a Gaia TV course and studied several books by Joe Dispenza, focusing my efforts on meditations using consciousness to manifest and create the life I desired. And I have also learned much from courses offered by Ascension teacher Inelia Benz.

In 2021, I received a Quantum Healing Hypnosis Therapy session during the time I was taking a Farsight remote viewing course that is free on YouTube. During the QHHT session,

I connected with a Pleiadian being named Mira. She told me that she was part of the Pleiadian team working with humans who wanted to upgrade their psychic abilities and spiritual skills as part of Earth's transition to 5D. She has since confirmed that she was working with the group of Pleiadians I originally connected with while at Tiwanaku. I worked with Mira while practicing channeling sessions with friends and family. Although I still occasionally speak with Mira and can connect with numerous beings of love and light when I channel, I've found that the best results for helping people grow come when asking to speak directly to the Sacred Higher Self of the person I'm conducting the session for.

In 2022, Tracy and I went on a month-long tour of sacred sites in Egypt with Lee Carroll (check out photos of this amazing adventure). My channeling abilities soared during this trip as I asked for and received incredible energetic downloads every day from the pyramids and temples we visited. Since I was with a fairly large group of people who were traveling with a world-renowned channel, I took the opportunity to put my abilities to the test. I wanted to see if my channeling skills would be helpful to people accustomed to hearing from a respected channel like Lee. I was both nervous and excited that I would be "coming out" amid people who had advanced spiritual and psychic abilities. While relaxing on our Nile River cruise ships in between temple visits, I began offering channeling sessions. After each session I would ask the person I channeled for if their session was "useful." One hundred percent agreed it was.

Upon my return to Santa Fe, I was strongly called by my Sacred Higher Self to share my healing wisdom with the public. Because of the confirmation I received from folks on the Egypt tour, I could no longer deny my abilities or hide behind the self-doubt and fear that I was simply making this stuff up.

Over the past year I've provided Channeled Spiritual Coaching and clearing sessions to hundreds of people. You've read about the results of some of those sessions throughout this book. Now Spirit has asked me to get bigger. About the people who contact me are manifesting awakening and 5D skills spontaneously. They're mostly looking for another person they can talk to about what's happening to them. About one in ten who reach out tell me they'd like to find a way to do what I'm doing and help others step across the densities by ascending. And nearly everyone who books a session needs clearing work to move forward. They all sense they're ready for their next step, they just don't know how to take it.

That's why I've written this book, and plan on writing the next two in this series. This book is here to extend a helping hand to everyone reaching out for it. The final book will teach how you can be a person who provides this help to others. I'm holding the vision with intense gratitude that in a few years thousands of us will be able to provide one on one help to family, friends, neighbors and clients who are right where you're at now.

And here we are.